SABU

Michael LAWRENCE

A BFI book published by Palgrave Macmillan

© Michael Lawrence 2014

All rights reserved. No reproduction, copy or transmission of this publication may be made without written permission. No portion of this publication may be reproduced, copied or transmitted save with written permission or in accordance with the provisions of the Copyright, Designs and Patents Act 1988, or under the terms of any licence permitting limited copying issued by the Copyright Licensing Agency, Saffron House, 6–10 Kirby Street, London EC1N 8TS. Any person who does any unauthorised act in relation to this publication may be liable to criminal prosecution and civil claims for damages.

The author has asserted his right to be identified as the author of this work in accordance with the Copyright, Designs and Patents Act 1988.

First published in 2014 by
PALGRAVE MACMILLAN

on behalf of the

BRITISH FILM INSTITUTE
21 Stephen Street, London W1T 1LN
www.bfi.org.uk

There's more to discover about film and television through the BFI. Our world-renowned archive, cinemas, festivals, films, publications and learning resources are here to inspire you.

Palgrave Macmillan in the UK is an imprint of Macmillan Publishers Limited, registered in England, company number 785998, of Houndmills, Basingstoke, Hampshire RG21 6XS. Palgrave Macmillan in the US is a division of St Martin's Press LLC, 175 Fifth Avenue, New York, NY 10010. Palgrave Macmillan is the global academic imprint of the above companies and has companies and representatives throughout the world. Palgrave® and Macmillan® are registered trademarks in the United States, the United Kingdom, Europe and other countries.

Cover images: (front) *Elephant Boy* (Robert J. Flaherty, 1937), London Film Productions; (back, from top) *The Drum* (Zoltan Korda, 1938), London Film Productions; uncredited
Designed by couch

Set by Cambrian Typesetters, Camberley, Surrey
Printed in China

This book is printed on paper suitable for recycling and made from fully managed and sustained forest sources. Logging, pulping and manufacturing processes are expected to conform to the environmental regulations of the country of origin.

British Library Cataloguing-in-Publication Data
A catalogue record for this book is available from the British Library
A catalog record for this book is available from the Library of Congress

ISBN 978-1-84457-455-1 (pb)
ISBN 978-1-84457-519-0 (hb)

CONTENTS

Acknowledgments iv

Introduction 1

1 **'Starring' Sabu** 7

2 **Technicolor** 45

3 **Camp** 71

4 **Trash** 91

Notes 114

Bibliography 131

Filmography 143

Index 144

Acknowledgments

I would like to thank Catherine Grant, Lee Grieveson and Karen Lury for their encouragement and advice. For assistance with archives, I am grateful to Jonny Davies, Anastasia Kerameos and Martin G. Stockham. Thanks also to Samuel Solomon and Ryan Powell. The BFI and Palgrave Macmillan have been incredibly supportive throughout the writing of this book; particular gratitude is owed to Rebecca Barden, Jenni Burnell, Sophia Contento, Lucinda Knight and Chantal Latchford. This book is dedicated to John David Rhodes.

Introduction

A genie has flown our hero far away to a foreboding temple. Inside, the brave youth must climb across a gigantic spider's web in order to collect a mysterious and magical jewel. This Herculean labour will require courage, perseverance, dexterity, agility and strength; the job at hand depends on a supreme determination, a conscious deliberation, and even a kind of dedication. Indeed, several times he almost loses his grip, but hangs on, dangling above the dangerous drop. Two malevolent-looking octopuses are sloshing and swirling about in a pool a hundred feet beneath him, as if set on a slow spin cycle. Then, suddenly, the spider appears, bristling, bustling and descending with mechanical menace towards where our hero is perched. Dauntlessly, the boy uses his sword to hack off several of the spider's legs, all the while maintaining his hold on the web with his other hand. And finally, once he has defeated the monstrous spider, he uses its silk to swing nimbly away to safety, and thence to retrieve the jewel. This is just another exciting adventure for Abu, the intrepid little hero at the centre of the dazzling fantasy that is *The Thief of Bagdad* (1940); but, moreover, it is all in a day's work for Sabu, the actor and star who is the focus of this book.

Sabu was unique: the only Indian film star to be produced in and by the west during cinema's classical period. Born near Mysore in South India in 1924, he was to become an international star at the age of twelve, and remained an exceptional presence in the industries in which he worked, first in Britain and then in the United States. His Indian origins and identity were central to his public image and popular appeal throughout his career; he was undoubtedly presented and regarded as an 'exotic' figure. Sabu was inevitably constructed by the media and perceived by audiences in ways that reflected what were in those days widespread beliefs and ordinary ideas about 'far-off' lands and 'primitive' peoples, popular fantasies and ideological attitudes about India and Indians specifically, but also about 'the East' or 'the Orient' more generally. The constructions and perceptions of his Indian or Eastern identity were necessarily informed by their precise national, historical

Sabu as Abu in *The Thief of Bagdad* (1940)

and political contexts: his international stardom and transnational career coincided not only with the end of British colonial rule in India but also with the repeal of anti-Asian legislation (barring 'Hindus' from citizenship rights) in the United States. Just as important for an understanding of Sabu's career, however, are the technological contexts shaping the film industries in which he worked, from the emergence of Technicolor in the late 1930s to the breakdown of the studio system and the rise of television in the 1950s.

In the films that Sabu made we see the trajectory of a particular star. Maurice Yacowar has suggested that in every film in which the star appears we can discern 'the precise shades of inflection that the actor's personae from other films bring to the statement': this is the star's 'fertility of cross-reference'.[1] Throughout his career, Sabu was more often than not cast in orientalist extravaganzas, island adventures and jungle thrillers; he played *heroes* – whether impishly playful or intensely powerful – but he was always associated with the 'foreign' and the fantastic, the 'exotic' and the incredible. The first chapter of this book addresses the story of the 'discovery' of Sabu in India and of his relocation to Britain, and the film that launched his career, *Elephant Boy* (1937), in which we watch an inexperienced or 'non-professional' performer becoming a child *star*. Chapter 2 focuses on the spectacular productions he made for Alexander Korda, which consolidated his status as a popular international star, and in which the vigorous performances of this 'exotic' teenaged sensation embodied, but also transcended, their Technicolor spectacle. Sabu's Hollywood films, made during World War II, and now revered as camp objects, were primarily vehicles in which his secondary starring roles were conceived by Universal to capitalise on the screen persona that had crystallised around the actor. The third chapter argues that camp provides another means through which we can restore to Sabu his autonomy as an actor, since his performances in these stereotypical sidekick roles suggest, among other things, an ironic citation of his popular image. Chapter 4 turns to the film and television work he did in the mid-1950s, when he was in his early thirties, in which we see the labours of the 'has-been' organised so as to reanimate, or resuscitate his screen personality, and to exploit memories of his earlier films for the purposes of a 'comeback'.

This book will explore how Sabu was represented and understood at the time, how he was regarded and described, and how the media – but also, and more importantly, his actual films – constructed and perpetuated an image for this unusual star that comprised delightful merriment, twinkling mischievousness, intrepid adventurousness, graceful agility and dynamic vitality. But this book also proposes that Sabu's work as an actor requires critical reassessment, for those qualities, which describe the attributes of a majority of his screen characters as well as prominent aspects of his public persona, are ultimately produced by his demonstrable abilities as an actor. The French critic Edgar Morin suggests that

> The star determines the many characters of his films; he incarnates himself in them and transcends them. But they transcend him in their turn; their exceptional qualities are reflected back on and illuminate the star … . The star is more than an actor incarnating characters, he incarnates *himself in them*, and they become incarnate in him.[2]

Sabu's popular image was undoubtedly generated and determined by those performances in which, in Morin's phrase, 'the actor imposes his personality on the heroes he plays', in which he expressed so infectiously his characters' merriment, mischievousness and adventurousness, and in which he embodied so supremely their agility and vitality.[3] In the incredible heroics and charming antics of his characters, usually presented in fantastic or at least highly romantic settings, we can, then, discern not only Sabu's sterling professionalism as a star but also his conscious and creative skills as an actor. Yacowar suggests that 'When Hollywood doomed a star to a succession of similar roles, it was instinctively expressing its sense that a film actor projects something somewhere between his self and his character when he appears on the screen.'[4] While it is important to consider the material conditions and cultural contexts in which his various screen performances were produced, it is equally necessary to attend to the performances themselves – as ostensive 'projections' that combine the particular fictional character, the star image and the actor's own self – in order for his labours as an actor to be properly apprehended and appreciated, and for his appeal and significance as a star to be fully understood and evaluated.

One of the first photographs of Sabu to appear in the British press, in early December 1935, shows a little grinning boy wearing a turban; it is captioned 'Elephants Like His Smile'.[5] The young star would indeed become famous for his smile. In his autobiography the Hungarian film composer Miklós Rózsa, who worked on several of Sabu's British films, makes a passing reference to the star: 'He was no actor,' Rózsa claims, 'all he could do really was smile, but this smile smiled him into the hearts of millions'.[6] Such a claim, purporting to explain Sabu's appeal, reduces the star to his smile – rather like the Cheshire Cat in Lewis Carroll's *Alice's Adventures in Wonderland* – as if this physical gesture alone were sufficient to sustain the public affection in which he was held, and so refuses to recognise other dimensions of his labours as a performer. In what follows, I challenge such dismissive attitudes by addressing Sabu's strenuous efforts and irrefutable achievements as an actor, while acknowledging the physical and gestural aspects that were often paramount in his performances. Indeed, several contemporary approaches to film performance emphasise its basis in actors' physical comportment. For instance, Jeremy G. Butler argues that until very recently theories of film have failed to understand 'the significance of human bodies – their movement and, later their speech – to the pleasures of cinema'.[7] Lesley Stern and George Kouvaros propose 'a notion of performance as closer to bodily action', in which acting is 'reconsidered and reinvested as a corporeal presence'.[8] For John Ellis, moreover, the *star* performance introduces

> a whole new dimension of the star: not just the star-in-movement, but also the incidental aspects of that movement. The star's performance in a film reveals to the viewer all those small gestures, particular aspects of movement and expression … . These moments permit a sense of overlooking the incidental and the unmotivated aspects of the star's figure (compared with the marked intentionality of the star image in subsidiary circulation.[9]

Ellis suggests that the pleasures of observing the star performance result at least in part from its revealing the star's physical being in such detail that we can glimpse – or at least imagine that we glimpse – the real individual 'beneath' or 'behind' their star image. Attending to the details of Sabu's performances, to specific aspects of his 'corporeal presence' and 'bodily action' in the films in which he worked, will enable here a reconsideration of his agency as an actor whose screen roles provided important opportunities for him to embody, endure, exceed and exploit his particular star image.

Sabu as Toomai in *Elephant Boy* (1937)

1: 'Starring' Sabu

When *Elephant Boy* was shown in cinemas during the spring of 1937, audiences around the world were finally and as it were formally introduced to the young Indian boy by the name of Sabu. *Elephant Boy* is perhaps the definitive Sabu film, and the star would be known as the 'elephant boy' for the duration of his career. The dominant contours of his persona were arguably crystallised by the promotion and publicity surrounding this film, and his debut screen performance would epitomise his unique attractions for a generation of fans. Contemporary reviews of Sabu's performance in *Elephant Boy*, and the features that appeared in the press before and following the film's release, inaugurated and established the vocabulary that would be repeatedly deployed to describe his body, to define his labour, to explain his appeal and to account for his success. By the time the film was released, numerous photographs of Sabu had featured in newspaper accounts of the film. The story of his 'discovery' had been told and retold many times, and it was widely reported how Sabu's participation in the production of *Elephant Boy* had totally transformed his life. The wonderful 'rags-to-riches' tale was repeated over and over again: until very recently he was a poor and pitiful orphan, roaming the jungles of southern India, but now, at the age of thirteen, he was a film star, working for one of the most important men in the British film industry.

Sabu's enduring identification with *Elephant Boy* was thoroughly constitutive of his star image and had a determining impact on his film career as an adult. Sabu was always associated with elephants, and with the animal kingdom more generally – with, in other words, the *non-human* – and also with youthfulness and boyishness – with, in other words, the *non-adult*. Consequently, the manufacture or construction of Sabu's star persona was in certain and important respects continuous with traditional ideological representations of colonised subjects, even though, or perhaps precisely because his rise to stardom coincided with the decline and eventual dismantling of Britain's imperial power in India. As the historian J. M. Blaut has argued, 'the coloniser's model of the world' viewed non-Europeans as '*undeveloped ... more or less childlike*'.[10] According to this 'model', these 'childlike' subjects 'could of course be brought to adulthood, to rationality, to modernity, through a set of learning experiences, mainly colonial'.[11] Popular accounts and representations of Sabu's early years in India and of his being brought to England at the age of twelve to become a film star invariably reflected the attitudes and assumptions associated with the colonialist model Blaut describes.[12]

Back in the winter of 1936, before *Elephant Boy* had been released, the *Times of India* reported that Sabu had 'become the hero of Britain's biggest film studio, and [was] one of the highest-paid actors in London'.[13] The newspaper explained that

> Sabu and his smile have become familiar to the British public both by their intrinsic charm and through a campaign of adroit press publicity. [...] His picture appears more frequently in the ... press than that of any other Indian and his personality is played up for all it is worth.[14]

The popularity of Sabu is here described as rooted in an innate appeal but also as the result of the deliberate manufacturing of his public image. The hoopla accompanying *Elephant Boy*'s release indeed revolved almost entirely around the vitality of the young star. Sabu's 'intrinsic charm' was emphasised from the start so as to differentiate him from the more obviously manufactured child stars of the period (such as Shirley Temple). The *New York Times* described Sabu as 'a sunny-faced, manly little youngster, whose naturalness beneath the camera's scrutiny should bring blushes to the faces of the precocious wonder-children of Hollywood'.[15] An image of Sabu – as small but strong, with an infectiously delightful smile, and an engagingly insouciant and marvellously confident screen presence – was established at the very beginning of his career, and this image remained affixed to the actor until his death in 1963. The palpable enthusiasm and energy that critics discerned in Sabu's portrayal of the mischievous and intrepid hero of *Elephant Boy* were to become the defining features of his screen persona, and his debut performance thus became a touchstone for the popular reception of his subsequent film roles. A sustained focus on Sabu's performances, beginning with *Elephant Boy*, in conjunction with an analysis of the construction of his public persona, will here provide the means with which to re-evaluate his significance as an icon. Attending to both the material conditions and the expressive creativity of

An early newspaper item about Sabu

He's a star, is Sabu, 12-year-old orphan, who acts Toomai in Robert Flaherty's film, "Elephant Boy." His father was a mahout.

his labouring as an actor will enable a reconsideration of his agency and autonomy as an 'exotic' star working for industries whose products invariably reflected the 'coloniser's model of the world'.

Elephant Boy is an adaptation of 'Toomai of the Elephants,' a tale from *The Jungle Book* (1894) by Rudyard Kipling (1865–1936). According to Wallace W. Robson, the most important literary source for Kipling's stories was 'undoubtedly the anecdotes of Rudyard's father, Lockwood Kipling, in his *Beast and Man in India* (1891)'.[16] Lockwood Kipling had devoted a chapter of his book to the elephant, which he described as 'one of the wonders of the world, amazing in his aspect and full of delightful and surprising qualities'.[17] In *The Jungle Book*, Toomai is the son of a *mahout* (elephant driver); the story concerns the boy's adventures with his elephant, Kala Nag, and chiefly his participation in an elephant drive organised by Colonel Petersen, a representative of the British government. Much of the material in *Beast and Man in India* concerning elephants was drawn from an earlier book, George Sanderson's *Thirteen Years among the Wild Beasts of India* (1879); while working for the British Government in India in the 1860s, Sanderson had introduced the use of the stockade (or *keddah*) for capturing wild elephants, and he is assumed to be the model for Rudyard Kipling's Colonel Petersen.[18] In *Beast and Man in India* it is claimed that *mahouts* 'tell and believe of the beasts in their charge more wonderful stories of intelligence than any in our children's books', and 'Toomai of the Elephants' draws on one particular legend, suggested by trampled areas discovered in the jungles – that herds of wild elephants often gather together at night to dance. Lockwood Kipling writes, somewhat indulgently:

Let us believe, then, until some dismal authority forbids us, that the elephant *beau monde* meets by the bright Indian moonlight in the ballrooms they clear in the depths of the forest, and dance mammoth quadrilles and reels to the sighing of the wind through the trees.[19]

Throughout *Elephant Boy* its young star displays both a bold confidence and an impish nonchalance whenever he is interacting with elephants, whether he is clambering nimbly up Kala Nag's proffered leg, riding the elephant perched astride its head or lying face down its back, or expertly washing him in a river, balancing precariously on the elephant's back as it slowly rolls over onto its side, and then vigorously scrubbing its ears with a rock. Several times in the film Kala Nag wraps his trunk securely around Sabu's body and hoists the boy up onto his head, and numerous international posters for *Elephant Boy* depicted Sabu as Toomai suspended in space, gripped by the trunk of his beloved elephant companion. Reports of the discovery of Sabu that appeared in the press always emphasised that the child was a '*bona fide* elephant boy', a 'real-life Toomai', and routinely claimed that there were extraordinary and even uncanny parallels between Kipling's fictional boy hero and the real child who played him in the film; this was said to account for the boy's incredible ease with his elephant co-stars. In much of the publicity for *Elephant Boy* it is often difficult to tell where one boy – Sabu – ended and the other boy – Toomai – began. For example, in *Sabu of the Elephants*, a biography of the young star published in 1938, Jack Whittingham plagiarises Kipling to evoke Sabu's formative years in the jungles. Kipling describes how Toomai liked 'the rush of the frightened pig and peacock under Kala Nag's feet; the blinding warm rains, when all the hills and valleys smoke; the beautiful misty mornings when nobody knew where they would camp that night'.[20] In the biography, we read how *Sabu*

knew the rush of the frightened pig, the weird peacock calls, the sting of the blinding monsoon rains, and the smoke that came up from the hills and valleys when the rains ceased. He knew the thrilling misty mornings, the elephant drives, and the pounding of their great wild limbs against the timbers of the stockade.[21]

The early life of a real child (Sabu) is here described by simply duplicating language used by Kipling to evoke the fictional child Toomai in his original and fantastic tale. Due to his having been an authentic elephant boy, however, it is imperative that Sabu be distinguished from Toomai if his performance in *Elephant*

Boy is to be properly recognised *as* a performance, and if his work in the film, his working for the film, is to be understood as his playing a character rather than his simply being himself.

The film which was to become *Elephant Boy* was originally conceived by Robert Flaherty, the American director often regarded as the 'father' of documentary film. Flaherty's *Nanook of the North* (1922) had established for critics the non-fiction film as a distinct mode of cinema, and also inaugurated the director's reputation as an adventurous chronicler of 'obscure' or 'primitive' peoples; the critic Siegfried Kracauer described Flaherty as 'the rhapsodist of backward areas'.[22] At the beginning of *Elephant Dance*, an epistolary account of the making of *Elephant Boy* published to coincide with the film's release, the director's wife and collaborator Frances describes their original ambition to present 'the adventures of a little Indian boy on a big Indian elephant in the jungles of India with all the jungle creatures', and then, by way of introducing the patron of this venture, asks:

But who could be found to produce such a film – a film that depended on a 'star' who was a mere boy, and a native boy at that, a quite ideal boy, moreover, who had yet to be discovered by some one of us somewhere in India! This needed a producer, it must be admitted, of no little courage and enterprise. Fortunately there was such a one in London. There was Alexander Korda.[23]

The Hungarian émigré Alexander Korda was, at the time, popularly considered the saviour of the British film industry. *The Private Life of Henry VIII*, which he had directed in 1933, was the first British production to receive the American Academy Award nomination for Best Picture, and it was hoped Korda would herald a new era in British cinema, with films oriented toward and attracting international audiences and thus competing more effectively with Hollywood. Korda had established London Films in 1932 and, in 1936, with financial support from the Prudential Assurance Company, opened the Denham Film Studios in Buckinghamshire, at that time the largest such facilities in Europe. He had first met Flaherty in Hollywood in 1929, but it wasn't until 1935 that they decided to make a film together, which was to result in *Elephant Boy*. The collaboration provided Flaherty with the financial support necessary to embark on a new venture, with the idea that the film would be a prestigious and profitable picture for Korda's company. According to Flaherty's biographer Arthur Calder-Marshall, however, 'Flaherty thought he could get the best out of Korda, while Korda thought he could get the best out of him; but their methods were so incompatible that they brought out the worst in each other.'[24]

In 1935 Korda had purchased the rights to the title of the Kipling tale, the main characters, and the story itself. Flaherty, however, was less interested in making a faithful adaptation of the Kipling story and more interested in producing a poetic portrait of an Indian boy's relationship with his elephant. Before Flaherty sailed for India, Korda insisted he attend several script conferences with London Films' screenwriter Lajos Biro. But once he was in India, Flaherty proceeded according to his usual methods, evolving a story idea through extensive observation and research. Richard Barsam claims that once the Flaherty unit arrived in India the director rejected the script and 'began random observation and shooting in hope of discovering a new story'.[25] By the end of 1935, Flaherty had amassed a considerable amount of footage. But by the spring of 1936, Korda was increasingly concerned about Flaherty's adventures. He was under pressure from the Prudential to manage his company's finances with more stringency. The costs involved in the production of *Elephant Boy* were considered an intolerable extravagance, and all the more so since there was little evidence of the picture nearing completion. In June the film-makers were ordered to return to Denham, where the picture would be completed. Karol Kulik suggests that Korda was 'by now looking for the quickest way to turn his investment into a conventional, commercially profitable feature film'.[26] John Collier was asked to write a new screenplay. The producer's brother, Zoltan, directed the extra sequences that were required to supplement Flaherty's footage; scenes involving rampaging elephants and man-eating tigers were devised. Elephants were borrowed from Whipsnade Zoo in Bedfordshire. Indians, on the other hand, were sourced from the East End to play non-speaking parts or 'background'. A short magazine article published while the film was being completed at Denham Studios referred to these extras 'queuing up for their pay at 10pm at night after a long night shooting'.[27] Working-class Indian immigrants living in the East End of London were indeed sporadically employed for the crowd scenes that featured in British films with an imperial setting, and were usually handled by local merchants acting as contractors. Around this time, an Asian and African Film Artistes' Association was established to protect the interests of 'Indian and Asiatic people' employed as 'film artistes and crowd'; there were almost two hundred members by the end of 1938.[28]

The film was finished in the winter of 1936, and released the following spring. Robert Flaherty and Zoltan Korda were both credited as the directors of *Elephant Boy*: the eighty-minute film combines around forty minutes of Flaherty's original footage and forty minutes of Zoltan Korda's supplementary material. The men shared the Best Director prize at the Venice Film Festival in 1937. Alexander Korda had intended his collaboration with Flaherty to confer precisely this kind of acclaim and recognition on London Films, and the award suggested the project had been a worthwhile venture in this respect. For Flaherty, however, not only was *Elephant Boy* unlike the picture he had originally intended to make, it was precisely the kind of picture he had set out *not* to make. Critic Paul Rotha claimed '[the] final film shattered [Flaherty's] illusions that in Korda he had found the great producer who understood and believed him'.[29] Flaherty was thoroughly demoralised by his experience with Korda, and did not complete another film for almost five years. Despite its success at the box office (the film took around £100,000 – much more than all of Robert Flaherty's previous films combined), it ultimately failed to generate any profit for London Films due to the incredibly protracted production (the final costs of the film amounted to more than £150,000).[30]

'Discovering' Sabu

Elephant Boy was, of course, as Frances Flaherty had realised, 'a film that depended on a "star" who was a mere boy, and a native boy at that, a quite ideal boy … yet to be discovered … somewhere in India'.[31] In *Elephant Dance*, she explains how the initial idea for the film evolved from her and her husband's experiences working on his earlier projects:

Wherever we took our camera, from one primitive scene to another, we used the native people as our characters and took our material from the stuff of their lives … . So we had this idea; – why, if we wrote a film-story around extraordinary adventures that a native boy might have in his native environment, wouldn't it be possible to 'star' that boy himself in the film?[32]

During the initial stages of the production, Flaherty told journalists that there would be no professional actors in the film. Discussing his casting methods, Flaherty explains: 'What we do is go wherever there's a gathering of natives of any kind, and watch their faces, taking still photographs of any that seem interesting'.[33] When he is asked about the kind of child he needs to make his film, he answers: 'I only know that I want a native boy of about fourteen who has personality and character in his face – probably a lad who has worked with elephants and understands them'.[34] During the spring of 1935, there were regular reports in the *Times of India* concerning the film-makers' search for a suitable 'native boy'. One such article declared that the boy must not have had any film experience, and must be 'natural'.[35] In early March, after Robert Flaherty's brother David had arrived in India, two weeks ahead of the director, the same newspaper offered an update on what is described as the film-makers' 'hunt'. Despite numerous applications received in England, it claims, the 'search for a boy skilled in the handling of elephants' is to commence in Bombay, and '[if] no suitable person is forthcoming, the company proposes to continue its search in the villages where the film is to be made'.[36] By the end of the month, the newspaper states that in their 'Search for [a] Boy to Take [the] Part of [the] Mahout's Son' the film-makers 'are now reserving their inquiries for the elephant country, where a mahout's son will probably be invited to take the part'.[37] Robert Flaherty, who had by this time joined his brother, explains in an interview that he sought 'a little Hindu boy who has not become sophisticated':

I am sure that such a boy, if we can find him – a happy, mischievous boy, the kind that typifies boyhood all over the world – will do an immense amount of good, by proving to the rest of the world that children are just as human and lovable in India as they are anywhere else.[38]

It was not unusual to promote films by advertising the search to discover an actor or actress to play a leading part. For example, David Selznick reportedly tested 10,000 boys before casting the British Freddie Bartholomew in the title role in *David Copperfield* (1935), and it was claimed that the producer's subsequent and widely publicised search to find a boy to play Tom Sawyer, which began in 1936, involved more than twice that number.[39] While it was never reported how many children were actually considered for the production of *Elephant Boy*, the scale of the search was represented in terms of the distance covered, the hundreds of miles the film-makers travelled – as far as Malabar – looking for the appropriate 'native child', and the search was repeatedly described as an 'expedition'. The film-makers' quest to discover the whereabouts of their 'little Hindu boy' thus became a kind of imperial adventure, an epic and romantic treasure hunt. The story of the hunt for the child to play the lead role in the film resonates with the story of the search for the wild elephants that would eventually form the basis of the film. In *Elephant Boy*, the elephants are sought because of

Osmond Borradaile shooting *Elephant Boy* in India

the value of their physical strength, because they can be trained to work for adults. The search for a 'natural' Indian child would result in the discovery of a boy whose real value would emerge only after he began working for the adult film-makers responsible for producing the film.

By May of 1935, Flaherty's 'expedition' had moved to southern India, where the Maharajah of Mysore put at the film-makers' disposal one of his empty palaces, the Chittaranjana Mahal, and offered them the use of his own collection of elephants. Eventually it was decided to shoot the film in Mysore and the palace was subsequently converted into a base for their operations.[40] In a letter dated 25 May, Frances Flaherty admits 'We haven't found our "Toomai" yet.'[41] Frances reflects on the 'various candidates' she had begun to observe in the vicinity. She writes, 'I watch them playing around, kicking a football, shouting and fighting like kids everywhere, and think of the strange stroke of fate that is hanging over one of them.'[42] It was Flaherty's cinematographer who first presented to the director and his wife a child he had observed lolling about at the Maharajah's elephant stables. According to Osmond Borradaile's account, written many decades later, he had been instantaneously captivated by the boy's 'fine physique and grace of movement'.[43] Borradaile recalls how '[his] alert eyes, ready smile, strong body, and forthright manner made him a most attractive youngster'.[44] However, he was concerned that the boy's clothes were too tatty, and his body too dirty, to make a suitable impression on the director. He writes,

Anticipating the importance of their encounter, I gave Sabu a few rupees and told him to throw away the rags he was wearing, buy a new *dhoti*, have a bath, and report to me at the hotel in the morning.[45]

The next morning, Borradaile remembers, the child returned 'spruced up and resplendent in a new *dhoti* and crimson *puggaree*' and wearing 'an infectiously broad grin that would endear him to film audiences everywhere'.[46] Frances Flaherty thought that Borradaile's boy was 'different from the other sprightly little sprouts' but noted that she thought he was 'rather pathetic' and 'more reserved'.[47] Robert himself described similar impressions:

He was rather pathetic-looking, and terribly shy ... . Though he ... was a *bona fide* elephant boy, his late father having been one of the Maharajah's mahouts, we hadn't the slightest idea at the time of being able to use him, as we were sure that the other boys we had on hand were much better.[48]

The film unit travelled to the Kakankote jungles to take footage of some elephants. At the last minute, Robert Flaherty decided to take Sabu with them. In a letter dated 4 July 1935, Frances writes that Sabu was 'gradually eclipsing three other boys for the part of Toomai'.[49] She describes him as 'so busy and happy showing us what he could do' and refers to his telling them 'I am here to serve the masters'.[50] Robert Flaherty claimed he thought that Sabu 'was already feeling his importance among us and that he realized, boy though he was, that here was his first great opportunity'.[51] While at Karapur they gave the boy a screen test. Frances explains that

> when we fussed with him over his costume, pulled him and poked him, tucked up his *dhoti* and wound and re-wound his *puggaree* (making him look worse and worse, I must confess), he took charge of the matter himself and told *us* what *he* wanted. He came out finally before the camera and all of us, as we stood around staring, perfectly business-like, self-contained, serious, not a child at all.[52]

Robert Flaherty recalled, '[we] put him into a jungle costume and made some tests. He walked as gracefully as a Polynesian, and even at this, his first time before the camera, was natural and free, with a smile like a sunrise.'[53] In Frances's words, '[there] was no longer any doubt who was to be our elephant boy', and shortly afterwards, they decided to cast Sabu in the film.[54] Flaherty began shooting footage for the film in July 1935. Frances describes how 'Sabu, his little brown body in nothing but a tight-fitting breech cloth, was a perfect thing of beauty'.[55]

The *Times of India*, reporting on the progress of *Elephant Boy* in February 1936, made a bold prediction: the film

> promises to bring to the screen a new Indian film star who is likely to become a rival to Miss Shirley Temple and all the other precocious geniuses. The star is Sabu, a ten-year-old orphan boy whom Mr Flaherty found in the Mysore stables helping to look after the elephants. The producer declares that his naturalness makes him a magnificent actor and his wide-mouthed smile has already been reproduced in the London press.[56]

It is the 'naturalness' of Sabu's performance in the film that will apparently distinguish him from other popular child stars, such as Temple. Hollywood's child actors, and especially its child stars, were regularly criticised for being too

precocious, too accomplished and too artificial. Typical of such complaints is a reader's letter printed in *Film Pictorial* in the summer of 1936. 'Heaven save our screen entertainment from a swarm of "clever" child stars' writes (Miss) M. Spiller, of Aberavon, who goes on to state:

> We have never yet seen a perfectly natural and sincere performance by a child star ... . They are fully conscious of their ability and know the expression and emotions to register. Thus all trace of naturalness is gone ... . The affected posturing and lispings of 'child wonders' is [sic] one of the most nauseating features of the cinema today.[57]

The same language is used in 'Celluloid Children', an article by Winifred Holmes, a child psychologist, which featured on the cover of *World Film News* the same summer. Hollywood's child stars, she argues, suggest how 'we sentimentalize childhood in nauseating and false fashion'.[58] Children are made to reflect this sentimental attitude in films: the child presented in Shirley Temple's films is 'precocious and clever', and the child presented by Freddie Bartholomew is 'unnatural and sweetish'.[59]

The representation of the child in cinema reflects the demands and desires of adults (the film-makers) but necessarily depends upon the presence and participation of real children (the performers). The image of the child on the screen is produced first during the shooting of the film, when the labours of the child are organised before and recorded by the camera, and then during the editing stage, when the footage of the child's labour is selected and arranged for the final film. As we shall see, the representation of the child in *Elephant Boy* – the organisation of Sabu's physical and imaginative labours and the images of these labours – reveals the contradictory demands and desires of the adults who were responsible not only for the film's presentation of a fictional 'elephant boy' but also for the child upon whom, as Frances Flaherty stated, the entire film 'depended', the child whose body was the necessary basis for the title character. There were, from the beginning, conflicting attitudes about how the proposed film should be made: the film-makers responsible for *Elephant Boy* had different ideas about how to deploy the child for the purposes of presenting a character, and about how to organise that child's labour in the interests of telling a story. In Sabu's performance we can see combined two distinct uses of this child:

Sabu and his elephant co-star, Irawatha

Borradaile and Sabu

Flaherty's and Korda's. While Flaherty originally sought to make a poetic portrait of an Indian boy's relationship with his elephant which aspired to be as authentic as possible, the film was ultimately reconfigured around Korda's ambitions to present a faithful adaptation of the well-known Kipling tale which was intended to be a commercial success. It is tempting to view *Elephant Boy* – from its origins to its completion – as a contest between two men, the director Flaherty and the producer Korda, and the film-making ambitions that they each stood for. Sabu, the child at the centre of the film, inevitably becomes the focus of a struggle: a kind of custody battle is fought over the little elephant boy. The film's representation of the child, as we shall see, shifts back and forth between Flaherty's regime of observational (if not quite ethnographic) image production – which presents a 'non-professional' native child as a *study* – and Korda's regime of commercial (and avowedly populist) image production – which presents that same child as a potential *star*. Korda achieves control over the completion of the film: he not only assumes responsibility for the film's representation of the elephant boy, he takes charge of the child who played the film's titular hero. Flaherty was eventually obliged to surrender his Indian boy to Korda's company, just as Titania, Queen of the Fairies in William Shakespeare's *A Midsummer*

Night's Dream, loses her Indian 'changeling' to the retinue of her jealous husband King Oberon.[60] By the time *Elephant Boy* was released Korda had begun work on *The Drum* (1938), a spectacular Technicolor vehicle for his young protégé, and, the following year, he proclaimed Sabu to be 'England's greatest boy actor'.[61]

Elephant Boy

During the film's opening credits, the pages of a book magically turn by their own accord to show the names of the people responsible for the film printed over images of elephants at work. Another page turns, and there is Sabu, grinning out at us from inside the book, like a magical photograph. The edges of the book dissolve, and there is Sabu, still smiling at the camera, standing in a studio, before a blank backdrop. He greets us, in halting English, deferentially: he calls us 'sahibs'. He salutes us ingratiatingly. Sabu welcomes the audience to the film in which he stars. Or rather Toomai – for that is how Sabu introduces himself – welcomes the audience to the film which will present his incredible adventures. However, because characters in fiction films rarely acknowledge or address the camera, this prologue, in which Toomai explains a little about the story we are about to watch, inevitably functions for viewers as an introductory encounter with Sabu, the star of the film, rather than Toomai, the central character of the film. Furthermore, the deep breaths that Sabu takes while delivering this prologue to the camera indicate incontrovertibly the child actor's conscious and effortful work to perform this part, and thus function as a kind of excess. They do not signify Toomai's character, they are not the gestures of a performed character; they show us instead Sabu preparing for the work of delivering lines of dialogue in a language he can barely speak, and they suggest the effort and concentration that this involved. The first image of Sabu that the film offers us, then, is of a child who is very clearly working as hard as he can and to the best of his abilities, to do what is required of him. What is required of him is that he articulate and enunciate as clearly as possible in order to introduce himself as a potential star to audiences around the world.

The film then cuts to an image of an elephant. This is Kala Nag, the elephant we have just been told about. This image is from Flaherty's footage, produced in India. The elephant snuffles about in the foliage at his feet with his pendulous proboscis, while a monkey in a nearby tree watches with interest. Kala Nag discovers and uncovers Toomai, who was sleeping beneath a blanket of branches. Toomai sits up, stretches, scratches and yawns, while the monkey in the nearby tree does the same, scratches and yawns. Kala Nag also 'yawns', holding his trunk up above his head. Toomai scratches his chest, lifting up his arm; Kala Nag scratches at his throat with a twig clasped in his trunk; the monkey also scratches himself, lifting up his leg. Toomai honks at the monkey, and snaps off some sugar cane which he then shares with Kala Nag. Flaherty's Toomai is introduced to us as a wild child sleeping outside and on the ground, interacting or rather acting (yawning and scratching) in synchronicity with the animals around him. This child is revealed to us as an elephant forages for sugar cane; Flaherty's ideal boy appears as a nature child. Korda's Toomai, who we met in the preceding prologue, was revealed to us with a cinematic trick, a special effect, smiling from the page of a book, but actually standing on a studio floor, addressing an audience watching him; he already belongs to the film industry, and to the business of popular culture.

When *Elephant Boy* was released, critics identified its composite character and sought to distinguish the scenes filmed in India from the sequences filmed at Denham Studios. For John Grierson, the film signalled the triumph of 'the studio mind' over Flaherty's original conception.[62] He considered Flaherty's contributions to the film 'real and in the great tradition of cinema: seen, and with affection, felt', whereas the 'synthetic spectacle' of the Denham footage brought the film 'at every turn to an artificial, different plane'.[63] Paul Rotha noted that certain sequences were 'beautifully handled in the most sensitive Flaherty manner', but thought the studio scenes 'obvious for their gaucherie', 'crude and astoundingly bad pieces of film-making'.[64] The film's hybrid form, its combining of footage produced under such different conditions, was clearly discernible in the presentation of its young star. Indeed, Sabu's work in the film literally embodies the juxtaposition. Consonantly, many critics noted the composite quality of Sabu's performance in the film, and sought to distinguish between the work he did with Flaherty in India and his work for the Kordas in England. They usually much preferred the former and either excused or attacked the latter. For example, the *Times of India* criticised the sequences produced at Denham (and in particular the decision to cast British actors as Indians) and claimed that 'the best scenes in the film are those in which [Sabu] and his enormous elephants play and work together'.[65] For certain critics, however, it was precisely Sabu's performance in the film that compensated for the awkward juxtaposition of the Flaherty footage with the Korda material. The review in *The Times* claims that 'the film is at its best in the passages of pure observation, the undramatic descriptions of the Indian scene', but recognises that 'as there has to be a story, it is a great thing that the Indian boy, Sabu, plays the chief part in it'.[66] The picture's success was thus arguably dependent on the child's performance; it was Sabu's body and labours that apparently bore the responsibility for making the film's component parts a cohesive and coherent whole. If Sabu's personality was promoted to attract audiences to the film, it was Sabu's performance as Toomai that nevertheless functioned as a much-needed binding agent for the film's hybrid form.

Throughout the film, shots of Sabu taken by Robert Flaherty in India alternate with shots of Sabu taken by Zoltan Korda in England, and it is relatively easy to distinguish the Flaherty footage from the Korda footage. One method of doing so is to pay close attention, closer attention than the film would perhaps want, to the size and shape of Sabu's turban. In the scenes filmed in India, his turban is rather bulky, and seems on the brink of unravelling, while in the scenes filmed in England, it is much more compact, and is clearly more tightly wound around the actor's head. The turban thus functions as a continuity error, as evidence of the film's having been produced by combining the work of the two directors, and Sabu's work for those directors, in two different places and at two different times. However much *Elephant Boy* might attempt to conceal its composite form, the appearance of Sabu's turban, like the performance of Sabu himself, reveals how this film combines strikingly different approaches to making films. Flaherty's approach is suggested by the loosely tied turban, and is characterised by a comparable disorderliness, at least as far as Alexander Korda was concerned. Zoltan Korda's approach, embodied by the more securely tied turban, was of course intended to wrap the film as efficiently as possible.

Towards the beginning of the film, Flaherty's location footage shows Toomai riding Kala Nag through the village and then importuning his elephant to carry him up onto the roof of a house where some melons are waiting, and this is supplemented and punctuated with scenes filmed at Denham, close-ups of Sabu's face, shovelling chunks of the melon into his smile, and talking to Kala Nag, whose trunk snuffles upwards for a share of the fruit. The shots that show Toomai eating the melon on Kala Nag's head have clearly been produced in a studio: it is obvious that Sabu is inside, rather than outside, that, therefore, Sabu is in England, rather than India. The illusion that Toomai is riding his elephant in these close-ups is an artful contrivance, achieved, I presume, with some kind of mechanical contraption. Sabu's body rises and falls to suggest the lumbering gait of Kala Nag but no part of the elephant is actually visible in these shots. The film cannot conceal the fact that from scene to scene, from shot to shot, it shuffles back and forth between images produced in India in 1935 and images produced in England in 1936, between real locations and dressed sets, and, at least as far as Sabu's

'I salute you, sahibs!': the prologue to *Elephant Boy*, filmed at Denham Studios in England

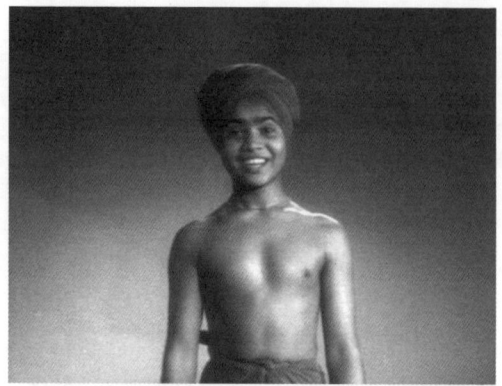

Sabu filmed in India, in a loosely wound turban

Sabu filmed in England, his turban now tightly wound

performance is concerned, between physical actions presented at some distance and lines of dialogue delivered in close-up. This sequence with the melon, then, demonstrates not only how *Elephant Boy* constructs its lead actor's performance by combining the original and the additional footage, but how the Denham material was designed specifically to provide for the audience a much more intimate and appealing closer view of the child at the centre of the film. The Denham scenes privilege Sabu's face, and thus appear to provide access to Toomai's character, while the Flaherty footage presents more objective views of Tooami's behaviour, focusing much more on his physical activity than his facial expressions. As such, the melon sequence is indicative of the way *Elephant Boy* presents a composite performance by Sabu, a performance that renders visible the very process of his becoming star. In this process, the close-up images of his face function both to focus the film more straightforwardly and more securely upon the 'intrinsic charm' of his smile and to intensify the audience's access to and identification with both the fictional character he plays in the film, in keeping with the cinematographic conventions of popular cinema, and the child actor playing that character, in keeping with the industrial system of manufacturing stars. Sabu's performance, unlike those of the actors employed after the production relocated to England, comprises images we might want to identify or understand as owing something to the traditions of documentary film-making – images that appear to capture a reality with authenticity and honesty – and images we might consider accord unambiguously with the system of commercial cinema – images that seek to fabricate characters involved in a narrative so as to involve an audience. For certain critics, the 'ethnographic' observations Flaherty pursued in India presented a much more effective (because more 'authentic') child hero than the studio scenes Korda filmed in England. And Sabu's interactions with the elephants, particularly in the footage produced in India, provided audiences with the incredible spectacle of a small child skilfully handling the gigantic beasts with what appears to be effortless ease. But it is arguably due to the film's focusing on Sabu's face, particularly in the more conventionally dramatic sequences filmed in England, that he is provided with a space in which to demonstrate a presumably more effortful but no less effective handling of his character's more intensely emotional scenes, such as his tremulous fortitude following the death of his father, or his desperate agitation and anguish when facing the prospect of losing his beloved Kala Nag, as well as those moments requiring less ostensive projections, such as when he wakes up and is at first uncertain as to whether he had actually seen or merely dreamed about the elephants dance.

It is clear that in the more dramatic sequences it is not possible simply to attribute the success of Sabu's impressively affective incarnation of Toomai to the fact that he was, as Robert Flaherty was wont to attest, 'a *bona fide* elephant boy': as I have already suggested, Sabu's already *being* an elephant boy when he was discovered by the Flahertys cannot fully account for the facility with which he becomes *this* particular elephant boy. The concluding scene in the film provides Sabu with the opportunity to demonstrate how subtly he could convey his character's emotions for the camera, and how capably he could control the 'irresistibly expressive' smile for which he was so famous.[67] After the wild elephants have been driven into and locked inside the stockade, Petersen (Walter Hudd) leads Toomai to where the mahouts have removed and orders the men to gather round. Toomai climbs onto a tree stump in the centre of the crowd and stands before them, some trepidation in the fidgeting fingers of his left hand. Petersen sternly reminds the hunters of the boy's claim upon them. The drivers agree to keep their promise – Toomai *is* to be a *mahout*, and from now on will be known as 'Toomai of the Elephants'. A close-up shows Toomai listening intently, his lips pressed together. Kala Nag and the other elephants are ordered to praise their new 'master', and another close-up shows Toomai's eyes brimming with tears, his eyebrows quivering, his lips twitching and then parting. Petersen invites the men to honour Toomai, and a third close-up shows Toomai surveying the crowd, smiling ever so slightly as a tear falls down his cheek. The cheering continues, and a fanfare begins on the soundtrack, and as the smile on Toomai's face broadens, his eyes, that were a moment before serious and even a little suspicious, finally smile as well. Then he suddenly sits down on the stump and hides his face in the crook of his arm, overcome by the adulation. In the film's final close-up, as Petersen's hand reassuringly pats the top of Toomai's head, he looks up, smiles through his tears, before shielding his face again. After the tumultuous spectacle of the stockade sequence, *Elephant Boy* concludes with this ceremonious honouring of the brave little hero. No longer considered a pesky burden, Toomai is rewarded for his usefulness (having led Petersen's party to the elephants) with the promise of a livelihood, and publicly recognised not only for his personal qualities – his bravery, loyalty and indomitability – but also as one who has been miraculously 'chosen' (for he and he alone has witnessed the elephants dance). This scene reprises and revises an earlier scene when the men had jeered at Toomai's ambitions to be a hunter, plonked him down in their midst, and mockingly promised he could become a *mahout* only when he had seen the elephants dance (a figure of speech equivalent to 'when pigs fly'). The narrative's resolution also resonates with the widely reported and 'incredible' story of how Sabu had been chosen to appear in the film and how he was now to begin a new life as Britain's most popular child star. More importantly, however, *Elephant Boy*'s final scene foreshadows the rapturous reception that was bestowed upon Sabu for his performance in the film. Writing in the *Daily Express*, Guy Morgan suggested Sabu was 'in a position to oust the [Johnny] Weissmullers and even the [Freddie] Bartholomews as the idol of every child in every cinema'.[68]

Karen Lury has suggested that

[child] actors balance precariously on the divide between seeming and being, and they continually undermine the belief that while performing as an actor (playing a character) this performance is held – not necessarily securely but importantly – as distinct from the actor's individual, everyday, off-screen performance of self.[69]

She argues that because the child is traditionally associated with naturalness and spontaneity 'the distinction between what is actually the "performance of character" by the child and its inevitable presentation as a "child" is particularly hard to discern'.[70] The Hungarian film theorist Béla Balász, writing in the 1920s, exemplifies this failure to discern 'the "performance of character" by the child' when he argued that '[the] acting of children is always natural, for make-believe is a natural thing to them ... it is a natural manifestation of their youthful consciousness ... their nature is play-acting'.[71] For Balász, this was observable 'not only in the human young but in the young of other species as well': the 'special charm' of children and animals was due to their 'unselfconscious seriousness' before the camera, and they subsequently gave an audience 'the sense of eavesdropping on nature'.[72] Most critics agreed that Sabu's 'natural' performance as Toomai was central to the success of the film, but their evaluations often accord with the ideas expressed by Balász, who, it is important to note, argued that the same 'play-acting' nature displayed by children and animals 'can be observed in savages or primitives'.[73] In *Elephant Dance*, Frances Flaherty had described how, prior to making *Elephant Boy*, she and her husband had 'found what good actors native children can be, and how appealing they unfailingly are to an audience'.[74] The responses to Sabu's performance routinely perpetuated such views concerning the playful 'nature' of the primitive or the unfailing appeal of 'native children'. The review in the *Manchester Guardian* declared: 'With his lively, black eyes and dazzlingly white teeth the boy is full of magnificent vitality'.[75] Another critic referred to Sabu as 'a brown frog of a boy' and as 'a shiny-skinned imp, with a flashing smile'.[76] The review in *The Times* claimed that Sabu possessed 'that natural and unselfconscious grace which can be recorded so well in a film'.[77] Sabu was celebrated for 'his sudden sweet smile, his earnestness and complete camera unconsciousness', and for 'possessing splendid photographic features and a healthy indifference to the camera'.[78] For the *Washington Post*, Sabu had the 'infinitely pathetic quality of naturalness that strikes straight to the heart', and this 'bronze and smiling juvenile' performed his role with 'the ingenuous charm of exactly what he is – a small and infinitely talented boy'.[79] The reference to Sabu's being 'infinitely talented' invites a consideration of his abilities as an actor. Lury cautions that it is important to remember '[acting] "naturally" is a skill – it is work. The child actor cannot be child*ish* – that is, irresponsible and unprofessional – about appearing to be child-*like*.'[80] We might recall here Frances Flaherty's description of Sabu's conscientious composure during his audition: 'perfectly business-like, self-contained, serious, not a child at all'.[81] Certain critics were more perceptive when describing Sabu's appeal, and recognised that he was talented as a *performer*: he was 'an engaging imp with a natural talent for acting'; he had 'natural acting ability'.[82] These responses are evidence that Sabu's performance in the film was certainly perceived *as* a performance, but they nevertheless also imply that his magnetism and charm stem from his simply being 'exactly what he is' (rather than his seeming other than what he is) and his being 'naturally' gifted. If the promotion for *Elephant Boy* had emphasised the similarities between Sabu's and Toomai's childhoods, it was nevertheless clear that by *playing* Toomai in the film Sabu's destiny was to differ from Toomai's in dramatic fashion. By starring in the film, and performing the part of the young *mahout*, Sabu had inadvertently guaranteed for himself an altogether different future – he would now no longer be an elephant boy (but, of course, he would also *always* be the 'Elephant Boy' of the movies). Sabu's subsequent screen performances, following his debut starring roles in *Elephant Boy*, were regarded less as effortful embodiments of fictional characters and more as further instances of him being 'exactly what he [was]' – or, rather, what his star persona, established at the beginning of his career, suggested he was: irrepressibly enthusiastic, innately amenable, effortlessly graceful and unthreateningly exotic.

Sabu's association with exotic animals, instantly established by *Elephant Boy*, was routinely and sometimes recklessly exploited as the star was promoted in the press and presented to the public. When Sabu visited the United States in

September 1938 to promote his second film *The Drum*, it was reported that he was briefly hospitalised after being bitten by a monkey that had been brought to the airport to be photographed sitting on the star's shoulders.[83] Vijay Prashad has suggested that the promotion of Sabu (and the films in which he starred) perpetuated popular cultural fantasies about India as a place that 'required animals in any representation for its essence ... to be truly realized'.[84] Representations of Sabu belonged to an imaginary that Prashad calls 'the oriental menagerie': 'In the gaze of U.S. popular culture, Sabu and the elephant appeared as specimens of India.'[85] Sabu made many appearances at zoos during the beginning of his career, and was regularly photographed posing with wild animals, both in England and in the United States. A photograph of Sabu that appeared in the *Daily Mirror* the day before the premiere of *Elephant Boy* shows the young star riding a camel at London Zoo.[86] Sabu was the guest of honour at the opening of 'Pet's Corner', the children's area of the zoo, which had been established by Julian Huxley, the zoo's manager, three years earlier. Sabu took with him his pet mongoose, Rikki, named, presumably, after Rikki Tikki Tavi, the mongoose in Kipling's *The Jungle Book*).[87] An article about the ceremony in the *Observer* noted the arrival of another specimen at the zoo, a 'bush dog, acquired by purchase from British Guiana' (a British colony in northeastern South America from 1814 to 1966, now called Guyana).[88] As John Berger has argued, the public zoological garden has historically functioned as 'an endorsement of modern colonial power', in which '[the] capturing of the animals was a symbolic representation of the conquest of all distant and exotic lands', and in which '[the] gift of an exotic animal ... became a token in subservient diplomatic relations'.[89] Sabu's appearances at zoos were in important ways continuous with the imperial logic organising their exhibition of exotic animals.

Newspapers also described Sabu's appearances at public zoos in order to emphasise his peculiar affinity with animals. In June 1937, the *Daily Mirror* reports that Sabu had visited Dudley Zoo in the West Midlands where he was allegedly 'reunited' with two elephants, called Ivahareneeu and Maharee, that (the article suggests) were his 'childhood friends': the elephants 'rubbed their trunks over him, bellowed their joy at meeting him again'.[90] When he was promoting *The Drum* in the United States in the Autumn of 1938, Sabu visited Prospect Park Zoo in New York, and was photographed by the press feeding the elephants surrounded by crowds of fans and onlookers. A news report described how 'Sabu,

(next page) Sabu making a public appearance at a zoo in 1937

the movies' famous elephant boy, yesterday looked over some of New York's behemoths', suggesting that the star's expertise with elephants authorised a spontaneous inspection.[91] Jack Whittingham's 1938 biography of Sabu concludes with the author accompanying the boy on a trip to London Zoo, where Rikki was spending the winter. Whittingham quotes his subject: 'You know, I think this is the most wonderful place in England', Sabu says, 'I like the sounds and the smell. I think I just feel all right here.'[92] Whittingham describes the star's miraculous ability to communicate with the animals:

> Sabu showed only too clearly, to the wonder of everyone in sight, his quite extraordinary power with the beasts … . He had forgotten his surroundings, and I do not think he was even conscious of the bars of the cages. He talked to the elephants in a language quite strange to us, but we knew that the elephants understood … . There hardly seemed an animal that did not respond when he called.[93]

Sabu's films repeatedly exploited what became the popular fantasy of his 'extraordinary powers' over animals. Throughout his career, Sabu played characters who were associated with wild and dangerous 'beasts' – from *Jungle Book* (1942) to *Man-Eater of Kumaon* (1948), and from *Jaguar* (1956) to *A Tiger Walks* (1964) – but it was, of course, with the elephant that Sabu was most indelibly connected. An American journalist, upon meeting Sabu in 1939, refers to how the star seemed 'a little bored at everyone's talking to him about [elephants] and at being obliged to meet personally, and ride, all of the elephants in the zoos of the various cities he visited'.[94] A report in the *New York Times* of Sabu's arrival at La Guardia airport in New York in the autumn of 1940 describes how 'an obliging but rather shiftless old elephant was trundled alongside the plane and a moment later Sabu was perched atop the pachyderm while the news cameras clicked'.[95] Sabu was thus obliged to become as 'obliging' as that elephant, and participate in such publicity stunts, because these obligations were integral to the maintenance of the star's image as the 'elephant boy'. Sabu's public appearances with elephants also involved the public celebration of the British Empire. In January 1939, Sabu was invited to take part in a procession organised by the Empire Tea Marketing Board in which three elephants carried six half-chests of tea from St Katharine Docks to Tower Hill, where they were then taken to the Tea Brokers' Association of London's headquarters in Mincing Lane to commemorate the centenary of the first public auction of Assam tea.[96] The

Sabu promoting the 'Sabu Ware' tea service

'oriental menagerie' to which Prashad has claimed Sabu belonged would appear to effortlessly overlap with an *imperial* menagerie, here deployed to market colonialist trade.

The promotion of Sabu predictably reflected and perpetuated the cultural constructions of non-Europeans that were integral to the conception and implementation of the colonialist project several centuries earlier and which remained constitutive of popular understandings of colonised peoples both in India and in Britian. The production and release of *Elephant Boy* took place between the spring of 1935 and the spring of 1937, in the penultimate decade of Britain's colonial rule in India.[97] In the representations of this young boy in the media, in the accounts of his having become – quite miraculously – a successful child star, we see how this process was framed in relation to an imperialist understanding of 'development', and a colonialist theory of 'progress', even as such ideas became increasingly anachronistic during the last years of British colonial rule in India.

'Civilising' Sabu

A typical article from 1937 describes how after several months in London, Sabu has 'adapted himself suitably to civilization. To see him dining with directors and producers is almost incredible, for only a short time ago he did not know what a tablecloth and knife and fork were'.[98] As Sabu was 'groomed' for stardom, and as this was described in books and in the press, ideological constructions of cultural and racial differences were inevitably mobilised. Indeed, in the various accounts of how this dirty, half-naked jungle child was transformed into a film star it is rarely difficult to detect attitudes that are constitutive of the historical project of colonialism. The post-colonial critic Bill Ashcroft has argued that of all the representations of 'the colonised other' that were deployed to justify imperial rule, 'no trope has been more tenacious and more far-reaching than that of the child'.[99] The 'strategies of surveillance, correction and instruction which lie at the heart of the child's education transfer effortlessly into the disciplinary enterprise of empire'.[100] Similarly, Ashis Nandy has discussed the 'homology between childhood and the state of being colonised which a modern colonial system invariably uses'.[101] Indeed, the invention of the modern concept of childhood in the seventeenth century, and the felt need to socialise the child through education, were, according to Nandy, instrumental in conceiving of the colonial project, in which the 'primitivism of subject societies' inhered in their 'childlikeness' and 'childishness'.[102]

An account of Sabu's childhood in India and his journey to England was presented to children in storybook form, namely, Frances Flaherty and Ursula Leacock's *Sabu the Elephant Boy*, illustrated with photographs taken by Frances.[103] It is, therefore, justifiable and even instructive to consider how closely the media's construction of Sabu's enthusiastic adaptation to his new home resembles another story, popular with children at the same time: *The Story of Babar the Little Elephant*, a picturebook by Jean De Brunhoff (1899–1937), published in France in 1931 and translated into English a few years later. According to the Chilean critic Ariel Dorfman, the Babar books were (and remain) 'primers' for colonialist ideology: 'Just below the surface of Babar,' Dorfman argues, 'there lurks, half unconsciously, a whole theory of development.'[104] His story concerns 'something more than a child growing up' – the history of this Little Elephant is, for Dorfman, 'the fulfilment of the dominant countries' colonial dream'.[105] Similarly, Stephen O'Harrow has argued that in the Babar stories 'the elephant exists in contrast to humans not in the way that animals really contrast with *homo sapiens*, but as certain groups of people contrast with other groups of people': 'Among elephants there are two subgroups: educated, clothed, civilized beings, walking upright and manipulating human artifacts; and uneducated, naked, less-than-civilized elephant/animal beings, apt to be instructed in walking upright and manipulating human artifacts.'[106] Significantly, the story of Babar the Little Elephant and those told about Sabu the little elephant boy overlap in several ways. On the first page of De Brunhoff's book 'a little elephant is born': 'His mother loves him very much. She rocks him to sleep with her trunk while singing softly to him.'[107] Likewise, *Sabu the Elephant Boy* begins by noting how 'Sabu's mother died when he was a very little boy, and so his father, who was a mahout (or driver), taught his elephant to rock Sabu gently in his cradle with her trunk'.[108] A couple of pages later in the De Brunhoff book, Babar's mother is killed by a hunter and Babar is orphaned. The Little Elephant's 'development' involves first leaving the jungle and moving to the city, where he is adopted by a genteel and very rich old lady, and then acquiring smart new clothes, driving a car, and excelling at school. He arrives naked and on all fours. Once he enters the department store, however, he begins walking upright. Babar buys himself 'a shirt with collar and tie, a suit of a becoming shade of green, then a handsome derby hat, and also shoes with spats'.[109] The old lady gives Babar a car, and after his morning bath Babar goes for a drive. Education also plays a part in the civilising of the little elephant: 'A learned professor gives him lessons. Babar pays attention and does well in his work. He is a good pupil and makes rapid progress'.[110] Dorfman writes that Babar adapts to his new environment 'by leaving behind the ignorance of his instincts, following the teachings and examples of the world that has given him refuge, and learning how to behave in the proper manner':

Somehow, without losing his animal appearance, Babar will be transformed into a polite and decent human being. He uses a napkin, sleeps in a bed, does exercises, has his picture taken, bathes in a tub with a sponge, drives his own car, and dresses in the latest fashions.[111]

As Ashcroft argues, colonised subjects are constructed and represented in relation to 'the possibility of an adulthood which will never come in any form other than an image of the West'.[112] Sabu was similarly characterised in publicity and in the press as having been 'rescued' from the jungles of India and as 'thriving' in the West by adopting the appropriate and proper manners befitting a metropolitan sophisticate. A report in the *Times of India* about Sabu's being installed in London to complete his work on the film referred to his journey 'from loin cloth to luxury flat' and noted that '[from] a shy, jungly youth, Sabu has become a handsome hero with a large income, a luxury flat in the West End, and a private car'.[113] Furthermore, images and accounts of Sabu's 'development', like the story of the Little Elephant, involved soap, smart clothes, cars and study.

A photograph of Sabu in the Whittingham biography shows the young star wearing a pair of pyjama bottoms, and leaning over a sink, about to rinse his face, which is covered in white soap, and turned towards the camera.[114] Anne McClintock has described how nineteenth-century advertisements for household soaps by manufacturers such as Pears offered 'an allegory of imperial progress as spectacle': in one such advertisement, in which a little black boy's skin is washed white by the soap, the domestic commodity is both invested with magical powers and made to embody the spiritual and civilising mission of imperialism itself.[115] 'By the turn of the century, soap ads vividly embodied the hope that the commodity alone, independent of its use value, could convert other cultures to "civilization".'[116] In March 1938, during the furore caused in India by Sabu's second film *The Drum*, a reader's letter was published in *Filmindia*, an English-language Indian film magazine, asking for the name of the lead actor in *Elephant Boy*. The editor answered: 'I don't know the real name of the boy but the matter-of-fact Englishmen finding the boy too dark thought of soap and probably named him Sabu.'[117] (The word 'sabu' means 'soap' in Marathi, the language spoken in western and central India and the country's fourth most commonly spoken language). The editor's response to the reader's question jokingly imagines that the white men who 'discovered' the boy desired (perhaps unconsciously) that Sabu's 'too dark' body might be washed clean, that his skin might thus be made lighter, made whiter. It is implied that the 'Englishmen' looked at Sabu and saw a dirty child who wanted a bath, a colonial subject who needed to be civilised.

Before *Elephant Boy* was released in England, Sabu accompanied the Borradailes to France to attend the film's official premiere in Paris. The *Manchester Guardian* describes how '[dressed] in a silver tunic and a raspberry-coloured turban, the boy made *salaams* and a little speech in his peculiar English to the Paris audience'.[118] The star's immaculate and ostentatious clothes, in stark contrast to the ragged *dhoti* which featured so prominently in both the popular accounts of his discovery at the elephant stables and in the film itself, suggest how for the purposes of promoting the film Sabu was presented as a kind of prince or maharajah. Whittingham describes Sabu's comparably opulent appearance before the audience at the London premiere of *Elephant Boy* in Leicester Square: 'He was wearing his bright red turban, his white Durbar coat of satin and gold, his black trousers, his patent-leather shoes, holding his whip and *salaaming*.'[119] The attention given to Sabu's exquisite finery not only suggests how Sabu's clothes were selected so as to suit an elegant, anglicised Indian, but also how the very state of being or becoming fully clothed was integral to the popular idea of his transplantation to England and his transformation into a star. Journalists were particularly interested in the clothes that Westernised Sabu: the *Daily Express* refers to Sabu as 'an Indian schoolboy in a new camel-hair overcoat, smart brown long-trousered suit with only a flashing smile and a red cotton turban to attract your notice'.[120] Such references to Sabu's dress, and to his dress *sense*, contribute to the idea that as Sabu becomes a star he ascends to a higher state of civilisation. A *Photoplay* feature from January 1939 with the title 'Civilizing Sabu of India: The Story of a Jungle Child in a Modern World' refers to Sabu as 'a slim, brown-skinned young fellow in a gray English-cut suit and scarlet turban' and claims that this 'rollicking Hindu child ... has grown into a poised young cosmopolite'.[121] Sabu's fastidiousness regarding his clothes was frequently described: a profile in *World Film News* by David Flaherty suggests: 'No star of the cinema is more careful of his appearance than this young mahout ... . Ragged as he was when we first saw him, he is now meticulously careful in his dress, always immaculately groomed'.[122]

From the beginning of his career, the media made much of Sabu's interest in cars, and this particular enthusiasm enabled the press to emphasise how the boy from the jungle took a special delight in the motorised modernity of the West. On his first trip to the United States, Sabu was photographed being presented with a motorcycle by Carole Lombard. Sabu's ambition, it was regularly reported, was to drive a car. A photograph in *Life* magazine in 1937 shows the star at Denham Studios, behind the wheel of his miniature car. In publicity from 1938 it is claimed that Sabu has 'showed a great interest in all things mechanical' and 'handles his midget racing car with the same uncanny skill with which he once handled the giant pachyderms in the Maharajah's elephant stables'.[123] His interest in motor vehicles was often linked to his childhood in India in order to reiterate his rags-to-riches story: publicity remarked that as a little boy he 'used to dream of the strange automobiles used by the white officials in the city' and noted that his new-found fame – his relocation to the West – had allowed these dreams to come true.[124] Wherever possible, his

Sabu with his headmaster, Captain Thompson

interest in such machines was described so as to connect but contrast his new life (as a film star in England) with his previous life (as an 'elephant boy' in India): for example, one feature noted how

> Sabu has ... been allowed to drive a caterpillar-driven tractor on Roger Livesey's estate ... and soon the small boy was expert at handling the tractor and pulling out enormous logs as he had been in similar tree-felling operations with a gang of trained elephants in the teak forests of Mysore.[125]

Upon his arrival in England, Sabu was enrolled in a prestigious school in Beaconsfield, Middlesex, and Sabu's devotion to his studies was integral to the popular representation of the teenaged film star as a mature young Indian man diligently improving himself through education. A feature in *Film Pictorial* about the making of Sabu's second film, *The Drum*, claimed that the star 'was the innocent cause of the location unit's few misadventures, which nearly resulted in the company arriving in Wales without its most important actor' – Sabu, so the story suggests, had forgotten that he was meant to be at the station because he was at school 'wrestling with an arithmetic problem'.[126] Jeffrey Richards has suggested, 'all the relationships in the Imperial structure ... can be paraphrased into an identical headmaster–pupil relationship along the lines of the public school'.[127] Representations of Sabu's schooling in England were able to perpetuate the 'headmaster–pupil relationship' between the coloniser and the colonised in quite literal ways. Whittingham describes how Sabu went to 'a school for boys from other countries wanting to learn English or study for the Universities'.[128] Sabu could already speak and understand English 'but he was still unable to read or write, and his knowledge of any of the other recognized school subjects was only of the slightest'.[129] The biography is illustrated with several photographs that show the young boy in suitably studious poses: in one such photograph, Sabu is dressed in his suit and turban, seated at a desk on which some books are propped open, and he rests his head on his hand, in which he grips his fountain pen. Another photograph shows Sabu with his headmaster, Captain Thompson, standing before a map of the world. Sabu is pointing to India with his pen and smiling across at Captain Thompson. Asked about Sabu's character, Thompson tells Whittingham, 'I think he must have been taken from the jungle at just the right age, bringing the best of what it had taught him with him'.[130] Thompson suggests that while in India, Sabu was 'taught' by 'the jungle', but it is clear that while this has resulted in the boy's 'amazing niceness', it is only a foundation for what can be done with Sabu at school in England. A 1938 profile of the star implies that his incredible progress is due to an innate need or desire that only his schoolteachers in England could satisfy: 'His thirst for knowledge is terrific, and he has learnt more in two years than a normal boy in twice that time.'[131] Such statements reflect a more general idea about Sabu's adaptation to his new home. As one critic put it, 'Sabu has absorbed western ways like a piece of enthusiastic blotting paper.'[132] Media accounts of Sabu's success and popularity at school and successful acclimatisation in England thus endorsed existing ideas about his 'natural' aptitude and 'intrinsic charm', but also used the star to perpetuate an imperialist fantasy in which the 'primitive' colonial subject requires and then responds positively to Western instruction and enlightenment. As O'Harrow writes of De Brunhoff's Babar: 'He shows innate strength of character, but a character well-shaped and enhanced by a civilized education'; his 'goodness may be innate, yet it can only flower in the proper social surroundings'.[133]

If the many accounts of Sabu that emphasised his seriousness as a student, that described his success as a sportsman and that acknowledged his passion for technology inevitably perpetuated problematic ideas about this star's 'progress' (his being improved through his encounter with Western civilisation), the image of the star that emerged nevertheless departed in important ways from the popular stereotypes that had been established since before the turn of the century and which were commonly used to represent Indian subjects living or visiting Britain. Shompa Lahiri has suggested that compared with other stereotypes the 'Indian student' has been neglected in analyses of the representation of colonial subjects in British literature and popular culture of the late nineteenth and early twentieth century.[134] Indian students had been a presence in British universities since the mid-1840s, and by the mid-1920s there were several thousand such students, the majority of whom were men studying law or medicine. Lahiri contends that due to his hybrid cultural identity, the Indian student was typically depicted as 'an incongruous, monstrous aberration' and that the 'most potent and abiding image' deployed was that of the *babu*: the pretentious, cowardly and effete, educated Indian.[135] The *babu* character, popularised by F. Anstey's articles for *Punch* magazine – published in book form in 1897 as *Baboo Hurry Bungsho Jabberjee, BA London* – presented an image of the English-trained Indian, speaking an 'excessively ornate and somewhat unidiomatic English', and mocked such Indians' 'impertinence to imitate traits which British ethnology has assigned exclusively to the English gentleman'.[136] The *babu* thus served an 'imperial purpose': the stereotype worked to neutralise the threat that India's National Congress was perceived to pose for British rule in India.[137] In contrast to the earlier *babu* stereotype, the image of Sabu the student was not associated with a ridiculous or impertinent 'pretend' Englishness. Furthermore, there were other aspects of Sabu's schoolboy image that functioned to differentiate the boy from the *babu*, particularly his prowess at sport. In children's popular culture, a somewhat less vicious variant of the *babu* stereotype was represented by Hurree Jamset Ram Singh, the young Nabob of Bahnipur, a recurring character in Frank Richards's stories about Billy Bunter and his friends at Greyfriars School, which were published in the boy's journal the *Magnet*. The characterisation of Hurree Singh allows us an insight into how the popular construction of Sabu departed in certain respects from the *babu* stereotype of the Indian student. Hurree, who is given the nickname 'Inky' by Billy and the other boys of the Remove, makes his first appearance in a story called 'Aliens at Greyfriars', which appeared in 1908, and is described thus:

His complexion, of the deepest, richest olive, showed him to be a native of the Oriental clime, and though he was clad in the ordinary Eton garb of the schoolboy, there was a grace and suppleness about his figure that betrayed the Hindoo.[138]

There are some important differences between Hurree Singh and his near contemporary Anstey's Hurry Bungsho Jabberjee: Singh is an excellent sportsman (he is a particularly skilful cricketer) and a trusted and valued member of Bunter's gang. In the 'Greyfriars Gallery' profile of Hurree Singh, which appeared in the *Magnet* in 1917, the author avers:

Who could help liking him, the loyal, good fellow, with his amusing speech, which yet does not make him a mere buffoon, for he has dignity enough – with his princely generosity and his brave heart – unselfish and cheerful, and ready of hand and brain?

In other words, while sharing some qualities with the traditional *babu* – his 'amusing speech', for example – Hurree is characterised by trustworthiness, good humour and generosity.[139] Describing his star pupil, Captain Thompson uses terms similar to those used in Richards's portrait of Singh (his remarks are included in the concluding chapters of Whittingham's biography of Sabu). Thompson says of his student:

I have never known Sabu not be white and straight, no matter what the circumstances or the situation … . He has never done even the littlest thing, to my knowledge, that you could call mean … . He never loses heart and he is never sulky … . His loyalty is extraordinary and he would trust a friend with his life. But if anyone every breaks their word to him, it comes as a most fearful shock. He simply cannot understand that sort of thing. I suppose it is all part of his innate 'niceness'. It is amazing how 'nice' he is.[140]

When asked where such 'fine qualities' came from, Thompson answers, as previously quoted: 'I think he must have been taken from the jungle at just the right age, bringing the best of what it had taught him with him.'[141] Features and profiles of Sabu routinely listed the many sports that the boy had enjoyed since he arrived in England: swimming, diving, tennis, football, ice-skating and cycling were among those described most frequently.[142] References to how the star 'plays football and tennis like any other small Britisher' suggest how for Sabu sports became an important index of how successfully he had adapted to (and also adopted) traditions associated with British culture.[143] But perhaps inevitably, Sabu's sporting skills were explained by his jungle upbringing: he was 'naturally good at games' because '[his] early training seems to have given him a perfect harmony between eye, foot, hand, and head, so that any ball game comes easily to him'.[144]

Media commentary sought to recognise Sabu's singularity, to affirm that he was an exceptional and unique star, but also wished to present him as a familiar and typical young boy. In her *Observer* column, C. A. Lejeune describes a young boy 'in his jodhpurs and crimson turban, lying full length on the floor of a suburban house, crunching toffee', suggesting how effortlessly the child combined the exotic (the crimson turban) with a typical child's insouciance (lying on the floor to eat toffee) in a cosy and familiar context (a suburban house, most probably the Borradailes' home).[145] The American Boy Scouts journal *Boy's Life* informed its readers: 'Sabu will delight you; you will accept him as a real boy of your own sort despite differences in race and custom.'[146] Furthermore, this perceived duality (exceptional-typical) was usually figured in correlation to ideas about his embodying elements of both the foreign and the familiar, the exotic and the ordinary. References to and representations of both Sabu's Indianness and his Englishness, moreover, function as fabrications, imbrications of facts and fictions, truth and fantasy. Of course, the images of Sabu that emerged at this time, the stories about Sabu that were told and retold during this period and the ideas concerning Sabu that crystallised thereafter, cannot be fully understood without appreciating their constitution by, and their remediation of, various attitudes and sentiments concerning both the history and the future of Britain's imperial interests in India. The emergent understanding, explanation and experience of Sabu's body, work and appeal that emerged during this period inevitably reflected certain aspects of the ideological apparatus underpinning the country's history of colonial exploitation. The starring of 'Sabu' thus suggests how national popular culture in Britain was suffused by an affective experience of the empire in the late 1930s.

The Times obituary for Sabu stated that '[his] story is perhaps one of the most dramatic in the colourful history of the cinema. No other child actor has achieved such a remarkable transformation from obscurity to international fame.'[147] The young Sabu is described as 'an eager, intelligent and athletic boy, of great charm and grace, who quickly learnt to act, and whose naturalness before the camera made his ultimate success certain', and it is then noted that the actor had 'an *obvious* flair for Eastern parts'.[148] The *New York Times* referred to how with '[his] white teeth gleaming against a background of smooth, coffee-brown skin and flowing black hair, Sabu captivated everyone who met him'.[149] In the following chapter, I consider the star's centrality in and significance for a specific period in 'the colourful history of the cinema' by examining the Technicolor pictures on which he worked in the years immediately following *Elephant Boy*. In these films, the 'coffee-brown skin' of this 'bronze and smiling juvenile' embodied the gorgeous vibrancy of the emergent technology of colour film.[150] But while the young actor thus functioned as a kind of 'talismanic' charm for the consolidation of Technicolor's commercial significance, the vitality of his performances nevertheless enabled him to transcend and perhaps even trouble the more ideological aspects of the films' deployment of the technology to provide exotic and imperial spectacle.

2: Technicolor

The three British Technicolor films in which Sabu appeared following *Elephant Boy* were produced as part of a July 1937 agreement between Korda's London Film Productions and Technicolor's Dr Herbert T. Kalmus. Korda was intent on experimenting with Technicolor as part of his ambition to make films which could compete with Hollywood cinema. Indeed, Charles Drazin suggests that during the late 1930s Korda 'played the single most significant role in introducing Technicolor to the British film industry'.[151] (Five of the nine Technicolor films made in Britain before World War II were London Film Productions; Sabu's second film, *The Drum*, was in fact only the third British feature film to be made entirely in Technicolor.) Sabu's association with Technicolor is arguably integral to his professional status and popular appeal during the late 1930s and early 1940s. Sabu's film career is remarkable precisely because of the number of Technicolor films he made during this period, roughly coincident with World War II. Sabu made more films in Technicolor than any other star during the period 1938–44, although this record was fairly quickly matched, first by 20th Century-Fox's June Haver, who starred in a succession of Technicolor musical romances during the mid- to late 1940s, and by MGM's canine star Pal, who appeared in five *Lassie* films – all in Technicolor – also during the 1940s. More than any other star working for the British film industry in the late 1930s Sabu was identified with Technicolor cinema and, after he relocated to Hollywood in 1942, Universal Studios was able to exploit its new property's association with the technology. By 1944, after appearing in three consecutive Technicolor films for Universal, Sabu had starred in more Technicolor pictures than any other actor. Sabu starred in six Technicolor productions at the height of his fame and popularity in which his labouring body, presented as an exotic and erotic spectacle, functioned to embody the Technicolor technology itself. During the late 1930s and early 1940s,

Studio portrait of Sabu to promote *The Drum* (1938)

the three-strip Technicolor process that had been developed in the mid-1930s was still inordinately expensive, and shooting in Technicolor was difficult, due to the size of the cameras, and uncomfortable, due to the lighting that was required. Technicolor was widely regarded as a fad or a threat, treated with circumspection or derision by critics and audiences, and with caution by film producers. According to Sarah Street,

> [the] historical context for the appearance of Technicolor during a period when colour on screen was unusual, invested it with an element of novelty which at times was emphasised by the industry, while on other occasions it was not privileged.[152]

Sabu starred in a succession of Technicolor films when the corporation was trying to convince the industry that it was a valid and viable technology for producing popular entertainment. This special young star, in other words, was to become associated with a colour technology that was itself both new and unusual, and his body became a vehicle for an emphatic demonstration of Technicolor spectacle.

In the mid- to late 1930s, the major Hollywood studios were rather hesitant to produce films in Technicolor, and were definitely cautious about putting established stars in Technicolor pictures. Technicolor knew that unless a major star personality endorsed the technology the studios would remain unconvinced. Most of the major stars at this time, however, were not interested in appearing in Technicolor films: as Fred E. Basten suggests, popular actresses were on the whole disinclined to 'desert the security of their monochromatic world'.[153] In the early days of Technicolor, then, Hollywood sought new actresses to manufacture as 'ideal colour subjects', 'born for Technicolor', who would then function as 'the major contributing force in "selling" the Technicolor process to the vast motion picture public'.[154] Basten explains that '[a] hopeful didn't require an imposing list of credits – but she did have to be colourful in her own rights, either in looks or personality, or both'.[155] Sarah Berry has examined the construction of a new kind of 'exotic' beauty ideal by the Hollywood studios during this period:

> One way that the chaos of the Technicolor palette was adapted to Hollywood norms of facial representation and beauty was to use performers whose style could be 'naturally' associated with bright colours' due to their 'exotic beauty' and 'colourful' femininity.[156]

The actors and actresses who did appear in early Technicolor films were discussed in the popular press in ways that emphasised how they were 'naturally' suited to the new process. For example, the Hungarian-born ballet-dancer-turned-film-star Steffi Dunna, who was the first actress to appear in three colour films, was profiled in *Film Pictorial* in the autumn of 1938 under the headline 'She's Colourful':

She is the ideal colour subject. Her olive skin, black hair and dark brown eyes provide the perfect combination for the colour camera, which brings the warmth of her personality to the screen in a manner black and white film could never do.[157]

As Steve Neale argues,

[whether] conceived and articulated in terms of the discourse of 'natural beauty' or the discourse of 'glamour', what was in any case both crucial and central was the inextricable interrelationship between colour (specifically Technicolor) and the image of the female body within the particular regime of representation and spectacle which the advent of colour brought to mainstream cinema.[158]

The image of Sabu's body presented by the Technicolor films in which he appeared indeed often abides by the 'regime of ... spectacle', which traditionally organises the representation of women in mainstream cinema and which, as Neale suggests, also defined popular film during the 'advent of colour'. Sabu's 'natural' charm meant that the star was already constructed by that 'discourse of natural beauty' that Neale notes became central to the feminisation of the Technicolor process. Sabu's 'difference', his exotic and 'Eastern' otherness, meant that he was doubly amenable and deployable by Technicolor's regime of representation. Sabu is perhaps the only male film personality whose 'natural' association with 'bright colours' – his status as an Eastern exotic – enabled him to become an 'ideal colour subject' for Technicolor cinema, but he was thus inevitably feminised in (and by) the process.

The actor was routinely described in ways that stressed both the colour of his skin and the colourfulness of his attire: the visual pleasure of contrasting colours is implied clearly by a reference to his 'dark brown features *richly* set off by the cerise turban tightly wrapped about his head'.[159] Compared with contemporary colour films, early Technicolor cinema tended to represent skin tones with much more density.[160] Scott Higgins has claimed that the successful reproduction of flesh tones was 'central to establishing the superiority of Technicolor' and 'remained the area in which colour fidelity was most valued'.[161] Sabu's 'bronze' skin was inevitably the most important feature of his embodiment of Technicolor cinema's bright and brazen aesthetic; it is precisely Sabu's 'dark' or rather 'darker' skin that is emphasised by the Technicolor process, and his difference was thus exaggerated and made highly visible. The denser and more dramatic flesh tones produced by filming in Technicolor were known in the industry during this period as the 'Technicolor tan': audiences were, in other words, particularly conscious of the complexion of the actor's skin when watching Technicolor pictures, and remained so until at least the late 1940s.[162] Richard Misek has suggested that in commercial cinema of the 1940s Technicolor was a 'prominent brand presence' but was ultimately 'unable to achieve its ultimate goal of imperceptibility'.[163] Sabu's prominence in early Technicolor cinema produced by both the British and American film industries must be considered in relation to a viewing context in which colour, and particularly skin colour, was intensely and palpably *perceptible*. Post-colonial critic Homi K. Bhabha argues that, in 'the ideological construction of otherness' through the construction of stereotypes, skin functions as 'the key signifier of cultural and racial difference … the most visible of fetishes [and] recognized as "common knowledge"'.[164] Bhabha reminds us, however, that 'skin, as a signifier of discrimination, must be produced or *processed* as visible'.[165] In these Technicolor productions, popular fantasies concerning Sabu's 'cultural and racial difference' are perpetuated by the stereotypical characters he played in the films, but, and perhaps more importantly, this difference is emphasised and exaggerated by the Technicolor process which the film-makers exploited so as to present, and process, his brown skin as a 'most visible' fetish. As Richard Misek observes, early Technicolor films were characterised by 'a technological fetishization' of their colour process.[166] In the Technicolor productions Sabu made for Korda, however, his sprightly and vigorous performances enabled him to transcend the films' fetishisation of their star's 'exotic' appeal.

In the 1930s, many commentators expressed concern about the impact of colour on cinema; one complained that 'with the screen a blazing riot of colour it is impossible to concentrate fully on any particular individual'.[167] Indeed, in his history of Technicolor cinema, Fred E. Basten reminds us that, in early Technicolor cinema, the colour process was often perceived as overwhelming the impact of actors, and suggests that in the 'magnificently produced Technicolor pictures' in which Sabu appeared, the star was 'upstaged by the colourful effects and surroundings'.[168] Sabu's Technicolor films deliberately deploy the actor's skin *as* a 'colourful effect' with which to display the 'magnificence' of the process, whereby his beauty, his body, his physical attractiveness and his 'exotic' appeal became inextricable from how early Technicolor cinema was organised and regarded. The vibrancy of Technicolor was perceived to enhance the vigour and sensuality of what one critic was to call Sabu's 'dusky athleticism'.[169] But while Basten reckons the star was 'upstaged' by the Technicolor spectacle, and other critics have argued that he was objectified by the process, close attention to the dynamic vivacity of Sabu's performances will show how he was able to transcend his 'talismanic' relationship with the technology and the popular orientalism it supported. Sabu's work for Korda following *Elephant Boy* is characterised by an ebullient vim, and an exceptional brio. More importantly, a focus on the expressive aspects of Sabu's labours in the three vehicles in which he starred for Korda will reveal the emergence of distinct personae and performance styles which were to have a profound influence on his subsequent Hollywood career as a contract player for Universal and as jobbing actor in the post-studio era. His starring roles as Abu, the impishly playful thief in *The Thief of Bagdad*, and Mowgli, the intensely fervent man-cub in *Jungle Book* consolidated the actor's popular association with, respectively, the effervescent playfulness of youth (the non-adult) and an intense allegiance with animals (the non-human).

The Drum

The Drum, Sabu's second film for Korda, was being discussed in the press before *Elephant Boy* was even released, and production on the film was underway shortly afterwards. The film belongs much more explicitly to the empire film genre than did *Elephant Boy*. John M. Mackenzie has discussed the 'extraordinary renaissance of the imperial adventure tradition' in the 1930s, during which popular cinema 'continued to draw its prime inspiration from a melodramatic and adventure genre – which best fitted the box-office appeal of spectacle in exotic settings'.[170] These films include *Trader Horn* (1931), *Clive of India* (1935), *Lives of a Bengal Lancer* (1935), *Sanders of the River* (1935), *Rhodes of Africa* (1936), *The Great Barrier* (1936), *David Livingstone* (1936), *King Solomon's Mines* (1937), *Four Men and a Prayer* (1938), *Stanley and Livingstone* (1939), *Four Feathers* (1939) and *Gunga Din* (1939). For Jeffrey Richards, the flourishing of this genre in the 1930s 'is a strong indicator of the extent to which popular culture on both sides of the Atlantic had become saturated with the myths and images of British imperialism'.[171] As Sarah Street suggests, the empire film attracts

Sabu as Prince Azim in *The Drum*

audiences 'by exploiting elements of spectacular epic cinema: lavish colour, exotic landscapes, large casts, horses, regalia, military trappings, native dances and costumes'.[172] In the late 1930s, the appropriateness of Technicolor for cinematic representations of 'Eastern Subjects' was assumed to be obvious. In 1937, one article claimed: 'The "gorgeousness" of the East, the popular idea of lavish splendour with which the average Western mind associates, say, India, is an association indissolubly bound up with colour.'[173] In 1938, a series of travelogue films presented the 'lavish splendour' of 'the East' in the still new Technicolor process: films such as *Temples of India*, *A Road in India* and *Arabian Bazaar* suggest how fantasies about strange and strangely colourful lands and peoples were transferred directly to celluloid through the strategic deployment of sumptuous Technicolor. In fact, one of the earliest and most popular colour films shown in Britain, the Kinemacolor feature *With Our King and Queen through India*, released in early 1912, had presented the Coronation Durbar of King George V in India. A contemporary review of the film is revealing of how the novelty and 'scintillating' spectacle of colour film were already associated with the East before the emergence of Technicolor cinema in the mid to late 1930s. According to this report, the film 'unrolls itself before one's dazzled eyes … like the slow unfolding of a jewelled banner', in which 'tones of scarlet and blue and gold and purple' are 'wonderful [in] their magnificence', before proclaiming that '[we] have often heard tales of the barbaric splendours of the Orient, but never before, perhaps, have we been given an equal opportunity of realising them in their full gorgeousness'.[174] In Edward Said's famous discussion of the 'invention' of the Orient, he examines the traditions of thought and imagery that have given it 'a reality and presence in and for the West': 'Orientalism', for Said, names this 'system of knowledge about the Orient'.[175] Orientalism imagines the Orient as 'a place of romance, exotic beings, haunting memories and landscapes [and] remarkable experiences'.[176] Such orientalist traditions were instrumental for the purposes of imperial propaganda: according to Richards, popular cinema at this time represented the British empire so that audiences might imagine the 'reality' of colonisation as if it were literally taking place in a 'mythic landscape of romance and adventure'.[177]

Korda's American distributors, United Artists, expressed confidence that *The Drum* would both 'capitalize the full box-office possibilities of Sabu, the charming youngster who fascinated millions of theatre patrons in *Elephant Boy*' and present what it referred to as the 'splendours of India' in 'the new Technicolor'.[178] The fascinating charm of Sabu is quite clearly perceived as belonging to the 'splendours of India' that will be fully and magnificently realised by the colour process: the young star will be at the centre of the Technicolor spectacle. One poster for *The Drum* proclaimed simply that the film presented 'Sabu in Technicolor'. When the film was released, Sabu was indeed once again praised as 'a charmingly natural actor' and, furthermore, identified as 'the film's biggest attraction'; in his new film, one critic said, Sabu 'once more exhibits his charming personality'.[179]

The Drum was immensely popular both in Britain and the United States, and Sabu's significance for the future of London Films was by now undeniable. In an interview towards the end of 1938, Korda acknowledges that Sabu was without a doubt his most important star property. He states that Sabu 'caught the public's fancy immediately', reveals that the star's fan mail 'is now about 100 letters a day', explains that producing new films for Sabu had become a top priority and concludes that '[the] main point is that the public wants to see more of Sabu'.[180] But as Whittingham acknowledges on the final pages of his biography of Sabu, 'suitable stories for such a specialized actor are not easy to discover'.[181] After the release of *The Drum*, in the summer of 1938, it was announced to the press that London Films would be embarking on an entire 'Eastern Cycle' of films. A screen version of *The Thief of Bagdad* was already at an early stage of production, as was an adaptation of Edward John Thompson's novel *Burmese Silver* (1937), to be directed by Michael Powell, and a film of Rudyard Kipling's *The Jungle Book* would follow: Sabu was to appear in all three pictures.[182] One newspaper article suggested that there were two factors that explained the producer's ambitions, one being 'Sabu's charm, an asset worth exploiting and demanding Eastern subjects to exploit it', the other being 'the demonstration which *The Drum* has afforded that colour technique has improved enough to make the most, pictorially, of India's life and country; and more, that a British studio can do it'.[183]

When *The Drum* was released, critics generally agreed that Technicolor was central to the film's achievements and importance. The *Daily Express* observes that '[the] mutinies, the massacres and murders ... are twice as thrilling when blood runs red and the revolver smoke is blue'.[184] More importantly, the Technicolor spectacle of colonial pageantry presented by the film was for some of a patriotic piece with its importance for the national film culture, and its achievements in Technicolor were of major significance to the British film industry. For the *Manchester Guardian* the film 'shows that a British company can provide spectacle, and spectacle which is in colour'.[185] A feature in *Film Pictorial* argued that *The Drum* was an achievement precisely because 'at last a British company has realized the existence of India', and '[challenged] Hollywood's right to regard India as its own property', concluding: 'Let us hope *The Drum* is a forerunner of a series of British pictures dealing with the Empire which is so close to our imaginations.'[186] In other words, the film's use of Technicolor thus functioned for certain critics as an expression, and as evidence of the nation's 'proprietorial' relationship with India. In *The Drum*, the British are presented as the only force adequate to control the warring natives, and the film therefore endorsed Britain's aggressive policies in the North West Frontier.

Ella Shohat and Robert Stam have suggested that empire films 'idealized the colonial enterprise as a philanthropic "civilizing mission" motivated by a desire to push back the boundaries of ignorance, disease, and tyranny.'[187] Indeed, as Sarah Street has argued, *The Drum* perpetuated 'the myth that imperialism involved "good colonizers" with a "mission" to introduce western notions of "civilization" to barbaric territories'.[188] *The Drum* subsequently caused much controversy upon its release in India: according to Prem Chowdhry, *The Drum* 'implicitly visualised India as a primarily Hindu India and made an ostensible bid at arousing latent fears of the Hindus against Muslim domination.'[189] Sabu's Muslim identity was often mentioned in the press: the very first reference to Sabu in the *Times of India* referred to the boy chosen by Flaherty to star in *Elephant Boy* as 'Shek Sillar, a 12 year old Mohameddan boy'.[190] David Flaherty's profile of the star, which had appeared in *World Film News* in April 1937, attributes the 'dignity in the little boy's bearing' to 'the mark of Islam', and adds that 'Sabu is fully conscious that Mohammedans are the best people in the world'.[191] It would seem that it remained important for Sabu to clarify his religion, particularly after moving to the United States, where Indians were generally referred to as 'Hindus': according to one journalist, writing in 1944, Sabu 'wishes it plainly understood that he is a Mohammedan, and resents being termed of any other faith. He goes to great lengths to let this fact be known'.[192] In 1940, the critic Louella Parsons would describe Sabu as 'a picturesque youth ... the only Mohammedan boy on the screen, and ... always the cynosure of all eyes wherever he goes'.[193] However, in 1938, Sabu was criticised in India following his participation in *The Drum*: the English-language magazine *Filmindia* suggested that the film demonstrated that the appeal of Sabu for audiences in the West was based on the 'imperial axiom' that Indians 'as a rule are unscrupulous and uncivilized', except for those who had learned 'virtues' from the British.[194] 'The popularity of Sabu in *The Drum*', the magazine asserted, 'is the popularity of a faithful dog or horse'.[195] After the release of *The Drum* in India, *Filmindia* accelerated its campaign to combat the production (or, at least, the distribution in India) of 'anti-Indian' films in Europe and the United States.[196] Baburao Patel, the editor of *Filmindia*, claimed: 'In his efforts to produce saleable pictures, Korda has produced *The Drum* at the expense of India and her hallowed traditions. *The Drum* is an argument for the British policy in the North West Frontier provinces.'[197] Progressive journals in the West were also critical of the film: the *Left Review* unequivocally declared the film 'imperialist propaganda', 'a sop to the decayed romanticism of the Empire's outposts' in which, it was claimed, Korda's use of Sabu amounted to 'further prostitution' of the child star.[198]

Several critics have argued that Sabu is presented as an eroticised object of the Technicolor camera's imperialist gaze, and is subsequently controlled by being made into a passive body for the audience to contemplate. Chowdhry suggests that the film's Technicolor 'highlighted brilliantly the natural contrast of the British and Indian skin colour, a contrast heightened by the image of Sabu's bare torso, which was maintained throughout much of the film'.[199] Priya Jaikumar argues that the film is organised around 'the voyeuristic display' of Sabu's 'dark body' and 'exploits Sabu's skin as beautiful'.[200] According to Jaikumar, the young star is here both 'commodified and feminized' by an 'image regime' in which the actor is 'softly lit, backlit, alternatively overdressed or semi-naked [and] frequently glistening': Sabu is, therefore, '[maintained] in a position of subjugation' even though the film '[admits] an erotic susceptibility of the camera and audience to his image. Thus historically, a commercialised pull of fascination with the native's image is concomitant with admissions of imperial vulnerability to subject lands and peoples.'[201] For Street, the Technicolor presentation of Sabu's skin in *The Drum* is linked to what she calls 'the homo-social, bordering on the erotic, attachment between Azim and Bill' and demonstrates how in empire cinema colour 'cannot consistently be contained within the realms of imperialist or racist discourse' and can in fact 'disturb [the] conventional, ideologically driven associations' which characterise the genre.[202] However, such responses fail to attend in any detail to Sabu's actual performance in the film, and thus marginalise the actor, assuming that there is nothing about his performance that might subvert or resist the ideological and technological visual regimes in which his labours are offered to the audience.

In this Technicolor colonialist propaganda, Sabu, Korda's most important property, is indeed deployed in very specific ways. His first appearance in the film is suitably spectacular for the production's top-billed star. We are in Tokot, the capital of an independent frontier state. There is a very brief scene in which Sabu's Prince Azim excitedly asks his father the King whether he can go and greet the English troops about to arrive in the city, and then dashes off. The troops are indeed approaching Tokot, and they are pleased to hear 'the sacred drum' being beaten to herald their arrival, but then suddenly they come under fire. The Prince charges towards them, riding a magnificent white horse, yelling orders over his shoulder, spinning his horse around once and then cantering off again to offer his welcome. The physical attributes – his small stature and his celebrated smile – for which the star was known and celebrated are explicitly evoked in the exchange Azim has with Captain Carruthers (Roger Livesey) which follows his dramatic arrival. Azim smiles, bows courteously, introduces himself, and says, 'My father has sent me to greet you, but please don't judge the warmth of his welcome by the size of his messenger.' Carruthers answers, 'I'd measure it by the breadth of his smile … if we hadn't been shot at.' Facets of Sabu's public image are emphasised in his character's narrative situation: the 'headmaster–pupil' relationship between the coloniser and the colonised, which representations of Sabu's rapid progress at school in England had invariably endorsed, arguably defines the relationship between Azim and Carruthers from this point onwards. The Captain suspects Azim had ordered his men to open fire; the Prince admits, with an irrepressible smile, that he had wanted only to see whether the English were as easily frightened as he had heard they were, but then is made to solemnly promise the Captain that from now on he will always tell the truth (or at the very least will try). Azim is presented as both requiring and responding to Carruthers's admonishment, instruction and example. In this first scene, Sabu's rambunctious and rollicking Prince is promptly taught some rudimentary 'virtues' by the Captain and, for the duration of the narrative, he faithfully assists the colonial powers in their attempts to vanquish the 'barbaric' natives. Azim's uncle, the evil Ghul, played by Raymond Massey, is a cruel bogey determined to foster ferment and conflict with the colonisers; his nephew, in stark contrast, enthusiastically admires, assents to and emulates the British.

In the film's final sequence, however, and following the successful squelching of the Ghul's desperate ambitions, it is evident that Azim's mischievous smile, which had originally been, for Carruthers, the sign that the Prince required reforming and restraining, ultimately cannot be so easily repressed. During the ceremonious installation of Azim as the new ruler of the kingdom, now officially under British protection, the young King is invited to inspect the troops. Sabu sits astride a horse, his arm raised in a salute, an austere expression on his face, befitting Azim's status. Then Azim's young friend, Bill, the drummer boy (Desmond Tester), looks up at the King and smiles. Sabu as Azim maintains a regal posture, but then his fingers, held stiff in the salute, suddenly flutter in a furtive wave, and he slyly acknowledges Bill with a surreptitious smile, before glancing to his left and assuming a more serious demeanour.

Significantly, then, at the very end of the film, a smile is offered by one child to another. Azim's smile functions as evidence of his irrepressible affection for Bill. The smile is perhaps inappropriate in the midst of such pomp; it is a secret and even a subversive gesture, a sign of the friendship between the two children that obtains despite the stark differences in their backgrounds and situations. However, when Azim smiles at Bill audiences are presented with another opportunity to see the famous smile for which Sabu was celebrated and with which the star was associated. Richard Dyer has suggested that 'the signifying

Sabu gives Desmond Tester a ride on his motorcycle while shooting *The Drum*

function of a star's image within a film' can complicate the actor's performance of a particular character.[203] Indeed, certain aspects of the star's popular image may work against components of the character they play and produce what Dyer calls 'resistance through charisma'.[204] The scene in which Azim surreptitiously smiles at Bill – like the earlier scene in which he smiles mischievously at Carruthers – invites the film's audience to take pleasure in seeing (the) Sabu smile, and thus to see the star image, as well as or even rather than the character the star is playing. In Sabu's subsequent film, *The Thief of Bagdad*, the 'signifying function' of this aspect of the star's popular image – the irrepressible delight of the child – becomes even more pronounced not only in the character he is playing (the sprightly and infectious Abu) but also in the actor's performance. It is precisely the dynamic vivacity and playfulness of Sabu's performance which enables the star to transcend and resist – through the charisma of his personality – the more eroticising and orientalist visual regimes with which he is presented as part of the film's Technicolor spectacle.

The Thief of Bagdad

With *The Thief of Bagdad* Korda reportedly intended to make 'the most splendid and breath-taking production since Technicolor was invented'; it was while making the film that Korda allegedly ordered a set designer, 'Rebuild it four times as big and paint it pink!'.[205] Charles Drazin has said of Korda's colour films that the Technicolor 'was part of the sugar coating that sweetened the pill of necessarily covert propaganda': the message of *The Thief of Bagdad* was that 'with courage, ingenuity and resourcefulness you can overcome a powerful tyranny' – and this was important 'as the bombs of the Luftwaffe rained down on [British] cities over the Christmas of 1940'.[206] Critics were unanimous in their praise of the film's achievements in Technicolor spectacle: the *New York Times* claimed that

> the particular glory of this film is its truly magnificent colour. No motion picture to date has been so richly and eloquently hued, nor has any picture yet been so perfectly suited to it … . The colour alone makes this picture a truly exciting entertainment.[207]

C. A. Lejeune, in the *Observer*, praised its 'rich, drowsy, candy-coloured, candy-sweet' spectacle, and called the film 'an Oriental bazaar of trick photography and Technicolor'.[208] Posters for *The Thief of Bagdad* proclaimed that the film was presented 'in magic Technicolor!': 'All the glories, romance, adventure of the Thousand and One Nights – woven into a thrilling triumph of motion picture magic!' The magic presented *in* the film (flying horses and carpets, marvellous genies and jewels) was continuous with the magic presented *by* the film (the special effects – 'motion picture magic' – that enabled the horses and carpets to appear to fly, the genie to appear towering over the thief, and all in magnificent colour). As Robert Irwin has suggested, popular cinema's showcasing of advances in film technology (including special effects and, significantly, colour film) was always integral to popular screen adaptations of stories from the *Thousand and One Nights*.[209] However, Michael Powell, one of several directors who worked on *The Thief of Bagdad*, was to remain adamant that the contribution of its young star was absolutely integral to the film's success; in his autobiography, Powell remarked:

> It was because the leading part was played by a child, and by such a wonderful, graceful, frank, intelligent child, that the film delighted audiences all over the world. Magical tricks and colour and vivid spectacle help to make a fantasy work, but it is the human beings in the fantasy who make it immortal.[210]

Indeed, Sabu's performance was acknowledged by certain critics as far superior to those of his adult co-stars: for example, a review in *Picture Show* states that

> John Justin [as Prince Ahmad] and June Duprez [as Princess Jasmine] make a charmingly romantic pair of fairy-tale lovers, but it is to Sabu, as the little thief, with his merry smile and mischievous glance … that [the] acting honours go.[211]

More recently, Andrew Moor has referred to the 'playground japery' with which Sabu imbued his character.[212] It is precisely the infectious enthusiasm and dynamic energy of Sabu's performance that enables the star to transcend the film's objectification of his 'magnificent colour' as a component in its 'vivid spectacle'.

In the middle of the film Abu and Ahmad (John Justin) are separated when their ship is wrecked in a night storm conjured by Jaffar (Conrad Veidt). There follows an extreme long shot of Abu lying face down on a beach the following morning. The film cuts to a much closer shot which presents a view of Abu from just beneath his thighs, and he slowly, languorously rolls over onto his back, with one arm remaining stretched out above his head, golden sand all over his skin. His hair moves a little in the breeze, his eyes are shut and his lips are closed. Then the camera moves closer still, affording us a medium close-up shot of the actor's chest and face, as Abu stirs and then wakes. These shots demonstrate how the film lingers on the surface of Sabu's skin: the first of the two consecutive shots that bring us closer to Sabu seems entirely superfluous, strikingly excessive, and would seem to function only to extend the sequence's gradual approach towards the actor's body. This arguably unnecessary shot thus serves to objectify the actor's body. When the camera moves closer the second time, it seems motivated by a desire to survey Sabu's brown skin at a closer vantage point. Marcia Landy has observed, the actor is photographed in the film 'in a fashion usually reserved for women and foreigners, in poses designed to highlight their physical attractiveness and to heighten the sense of sexual and cultural difference in a way that makes them exotic and appealing'.[213] However, just moments later, Abu is presented in a sequence in which he displays both heroic courage and Sabu his nimble dexterity, as he kills the gigantic spider in the temple. While the film undoubtedly includes scenes in which Sabu is presented as a passive object, to be contemplated as an erotic and exotic spectacle, it ultimately privileges his character as an active subject, to be admired for his athletic grace and ingenuity; the acrobatic Abu is very rarely *still*.

From the very beginning of the film, in fact, the little thief is associated with dynamic mobility. The first image the film provides its audience of Abu emerges as Ahmad recounts how he first met the little thief, who has since been magically transformed into a dog. A close-up of the dog's eyes dissolves into a close-up of Sabu's face, his eyes darting from left to right, and a smile dancing across his mouth. The next shot shows a fishmonger in the market turn away some beggars, and then the film cuts back to Abu, who would appear to be watching the fishmonger with a twinkling expression of bemusement suggesting he is planning some sport. We next see two little hands grabbing some fish from the stall, which then are promptly plopped into the laps of the two beggars, who look up in bafflement. The fishmonger realises what has happened, looks about, and there is Sabu, wearing a pea-green *dhoti*, leaping over a basket, upsetting its contents, and scampering nimbly through the crowds and across the square. The fishmonger yells 'Stop, thief!' and an alarm is raised. Abu pauses to lob some bright red tomatoes at the men now pursuing him, and then heaves the entire basket into the air with a grin, before disappearing again, bolting up one staircase and bounding down another. He jumps inside a large pot, momentarily bamboozling those chasing him, and then, after someone spots his smiling face peeping after them, climbs out and runs off again. He climbs up a ladder, and proceeds to jumps over the Bagdad rooftops, beneath the bright blue sky, laughing in delight. For this little thief, the entire city is a vast playground. This sequence provides a riotous spectacle of dynamic movement and comic incident, complete with cartoon-style sound effects (Abu's tomato missiles *whiz* through the air) and sprightly arpeggios on the soundtrack accompany the thief as he jauntily descends and ascends the steps. C. A. Lejeune, reviewing the film for *The Times*, listed among its pleasures 'young Sabu popping all over the place'.[214] With the introduction of its young star, the tone and pace of the film change, and its splendid but rather stately ponderousness is suddenly transformed — animated and enlivened — by his character's dauntless energy and mischievous joy, or rather due to the marvellous buoyancy of Sabu's performance.

While this sequence emphasises the little thief's (and the star's) acrobatic vigour, the next encounter with Abu presents him more explicitly as a Puckish trickster, and as a little *actor*. He is being dragged through the door of a dungeon in which Ahmad languishes, awaiting his execution. The little thief squirms and hollers in fear as the executioner is ordered by the gaoler to 'cut off his right arm, then his left, then his left leg, then his right, and then his head'. Abu throws himself onto the gaoler and desperately begs for mercy but is roughly dashed to the ground, and continues to writhe and scream while the two men depart. He listens for a moment, sits up, and then laughs raucously to himself. Ahmad presumes the boy must be mad, but it soon transpires that Abu is simply rejoicing at his own skills as an expert thief (he has just stolen the keys to the prison) and also as a prankster (his fearful agitation was only a pretence). The little thief here delights in the use of his dramatic skills to secure his freedom, just as he had in his acrobatic dexterity when he evaded capture in the earlier scene, and the audience is thus invited to enjoy not only the character's (and the actor's) physical vitality but also his (Abu's, and Sabu's) infectiousness as an adept *player* in this fantastic story. After Abu and Ahmad have sailed to Basra, Abu steals them some pancakes and then proceeds to scam them some honey by pretending to have severe misgivings about its quality and provoking the seller to give them each a sample spoonful. Later, on the beach, when Abu is about to be squashed under the terrible genie's massive foot, he tricks him back inside the bottle by roundly refusing to believe he could ever fit inside. Abu repeatedly resorts to wily stratagems of this kind, and the narrative thereby offers the audience numerous opportunities to admire the thief's resourceful playfulness. What results is an appealing impression of continuity between the exuberance of the character's behaviour in the story and the vitality of the actor's work for the film. Abu's intrepid heroism (and Sabu's impressive physical agility) and the thief's impish guile (and the 'playground japery' of Sabu's performance) refute those readings that see only the star's objectification by the film's Technicolor orientalism.

Like *The Drum*, *The Thief of Bagdad* concludes with a scene in which the audience is invited to take pleasure in seeing (the) Sabu smile. The city is rejoicing; the evil vizier Jaffar has been killed (by Abu), and King Ahmad has been restored to the throne, and reunited with Princess Jasmine (June Duprez). From the balcony of the palace, Ahmad announces to the citizens below that his faithful friend Abu will go to school and eventually become his new vizier. Upon hearing this, Abu sneaks off. By the time Ahmad realises that Abu has gone, the little thief is already standing on his magic carpet. He cheerfully explains that he would rather seek 'adventure, at last'. Abu waves, and smiles at his friends, and then soars away, over the city, and across the sky, beneath the arch of a rainbow. Abu refuses the obligations that adults have scheduled for him, and thus evades the obligations of adulthood itself by declaring he desires further fun and excitement. Asserting his right to remain a child, Abu delights in his departure, and dares his audience not to share in this delight. *The Thief of Bagdad*, in fact, finally demands that we celebrate this decision, and recognise this right. For some critics, the

Sabu as Prince Azim in *The Drum* (1938): with Carruthers

Bill and Azim

Azim smiles at Bill

Sabu as Abu in *The Thief of Bagdad* (1940)

Sabu as Mowgli in *Jungle Book* (1942)

Sabu as Ali Ben Ali in *Arabian Nights* (1943)

Haroun al-Rashid and Ali Ben Ali

Haroun al-Rashid, Ali Ben Ali and Scheherazade

Sabu as Kalo in *Cobra Woman* (1945)

Sabu as Abu and John Justin as King Ahmad in *The Thief of Bagdad*

innocent adventurousness of Sabu's thief was a necessary attitude to assume if audiences were to enjoy the film: Bosley Crowther, writing in the *New York Times*, advised adult viewers to 'be prepared to accept with an open and childlike faith' the picture's 'fabulous run of miracles'.[215] For Andrew Moor, the film 'insists that we keep a childlike vision'.[216]

In his discussion of children's literature, Peter Hollindale has considered the words that are available for describing children and the qualities of the child. He suggests that the word 'childish' is a term of disparagement, even when applied to children. 'Something is amiss with our vocabulary,' he observes, 'when our only adjective to describe children being children is one of disapproval': 'childlike', associated with 'condescending approval', is, he adds, rarely used to describe children.[217] Hollindale then discusses a scene in Shakespeare's *The Winter's Tale* in which Polixenes describes playing with his young son Florizel and comments approvingly on the boy's 'varying childness' during their role-playing games. For Hollindale, the obsolete noun 'childness' is a valuable word with which to refer to 'the quality of being a child – dynamic, imaginative, experimental, interactive and unstable'.[218] When Polixenes plays with Florizel, 'there is a transaction between them, a shared set of pleasuring beliefs about childhood and child behaviour, in which the adult can engage ... as a participant observer'.[219] Childness, Hollindale argues, is thus 'shared ground, though differently experienced and understood, between child and adult'.[220] Watching Sabu's dynamic and imaginative performance in *The Thief of Bagdad*, the audience is invited to take part – and take pleasure – in a transaction or interaction similar to that which Polixenes describes and Hollindale elaborates. As observers, adults in the audience are invited to participate in a fantasy that privileges the make-believe of children's play. And adults (as Crowther had advised) must be willing to access this childness if they are going to be able to celebrate Abu's infectious adventurousness as a 'pleasuring [belief] about childhood and child behaviour'.

Jungle Book

Sabu's childhood was regularly invoked in order to emphasise his suitability for the lead role in the film of *Jungle Book*: for example, one critic declared that

> Sabu was a 'natural' for the role of Mowgli, the young man-cub who strays into the jungle, is reared by the wolf pack and comes to know the jungle creatures. His boyhood was spent helping his father, an elephant mahout for an Indian prince.[221]

And of course, the star's confidence with animals was routinely described in accounts of the film's production: in the same feature it is asserted that 'Sabu ... moved among his unpredictable co-stars with astonishing confidence. Prior to production he had fed the closest of his jungle "friends" to remove the edge of strangeness.'[222]

Where *The Thief of Bagdad* presents a pastel-hued fantasia of open blue skies and seas and golden sand, splendidly opulent palaces and mythical creatures, *Jungle Book* is suffused with the deep jades and emeralds of dense jungle undergrowth and the brilliant orange of fire, and exotic wild animals. The film is much more fervid, more vigorous, and so is its star Sabu. According to one critic, 'the most successful aspect of this picture is visual. The colour and the sets are perfectly gorgeous. Those who show to best advantage in colour are Sabu and Shere Khan, the tiger': Mowgli, 'played by the well-built Indian lad, Sabu' is 'a Tarzan in colour'.[223] *Today's Cinema* also praises the film's 'vivid thrill and finely artistic spectacle, brilliantly enhanced by glowing Technicolor camera-work' and argues that 'it is the jungle spectacle which dominates, and the dark beauty of the forests and their denizens take on an added allure with the opulent tones of the Technicolor photography'.[224] The 'dark beauty' of Sabu as Mowgli is indeed emphasised by the film's Technicolor, but the dynamic vigour of his performance ensures he dominates, rather than is dominated by, the jungle spectacle: he embodies its 'vivid thrill'.

When Sabu first appears in *Jungle Book*, his head emerges out of the jungle foliage. His long black hair hangs down almost to his shoulders. His face, framed by ferns, prickles with perturbation. The narrator is explaining that for the man-cub 'every rustle in the grass meant as much to him as it did to his brothers the wolf cubs': Mowgli, we discover, is being pursued by Shere Khan, the tiger who killed his father twelve years before. A series of extreme long shots show Sabu as Mowgli swinging expertly through the jungle, Tarzan-style, before diving into a river and swimming to the bank opposite. A crocodile begins to course towards him, and, at the same time, Shere Khan reaches the river bank. Mowgli clambers out of the river and turns around to watch the crocodile and the tiger confront each other. A medium shot of Sabu shows his bare chest, beaded with water, heaving violently as Mowgli glowers at the tiger, baring his teeth with each breath, a fierce glint in his eyes. Then he suddenly swims away again, and an extreme long shot shows him climbing out of the river and disappearing into the jungle. This sequence invites us to admire the star's muscular body as he swings from tree to tree and swims across the river. Moreover, Mowgli would appear to be naked, which explains why Sabu is here shown either from just above the waist or else in extreme long shot. By the time Sabu makes *Jungle Book* he has become an intensely and androgynously beautiful adolescent, possessed of an admirable build. Sabu's physical development was undoubtedly the result of his enthusiasm for various sports, which was repeatedly reported in the media: the star excelled at football, cycling, ice-skating, swimming and diving. A feature in the *Los Angeles Times* reported that Sabu intended his Mowgli to be 'tough' like Johnny Weissmuller, and that the actor was 'eating beefsteak … so that he too can graduate to a super-physique'.[225] In an interview in 1940 in the *New York Times*, we are told how 'Sabu began to explain the intricacies of *jiu jitsu*, remarking that he could easily throw a man forty-five pounds heavier than himself'.[226] But the star's impressive athletic prowess, as displayed throughout *Jungle Book*, has little of the sprightly effervescence that characterised his performance as Abu. The vitality of Sabu's Mowgli is much more ardent: the critic Bosley Crowther, writing in the *New York Times*, for example, referred to the 'bestial intensity' of Sabu's performance in the film.[227]

After evading Shere Khan, Mowgli discovers a village deep in the jungle. He climbs a tree, and straddles a branch, clearly displaying his naked haunches, which are illuminated in the gloaming by the light of the village fires beneath him. Mowgli surveys the village with unblinking fascination, watching the villagers go about their business. There is a succession of extreme close-ups of Sabu's face, burnished by the firelight, shimmering with tentative curiosity, which alternate with shots of the villagers. The direction of Sabu's gaze almost coincides with the camera, as if to include the film audience itself in the human society that Mowgli is here observing for the very first time. As Mowgli watches the villagers, the expression on Sabu's face suggests that the man-cub is recognising that *he* is indeed like *them*, and that he might even belong among them. Mowgli swings down stealthily into the village, and slowly approaches one of the fires, but when he reaches out and touches the flames he howls out in pain. This wakes the sleeping villagers, who rush towards and around him. Mowgli barks at them, and bounds away, but they chase him, and surround him. He spins about, growling and snarling, and, when a villager grabs hold of him, he throws the much larger man right over his shoulders (displaying those *jiu jitsu* skills Sabu had described to the journalist, above). When Mowgli is eventually cornered, and restrained, he throws his head back and howls a long plaintive cry to the jungle. The villagers cover him up (he is still naked) and provide this 'wolf-boy' with a cerise lungi. Messua (Rosemary De Camp), a village woman (and actually Mowgli's mother) approaches him: she doesn't recognise him, but nevertheless remarks approvingly 'he's a handsome boy, with eyes like red fire'. She agrees to look after him, and leads him away to her house, where she tries to teach him the word for 'mother'. Mowgli cocks his head from one side to the other, like a thoughtful dog, but is unable to understand her. She asks him what the wolves had called him, and howls softly to indicate she means his jungle parents. Mowgli howls in response, and then haltingly murmurs his name – 'muh –muh– Mowgli' – the word (the first Sabu utters in the film) soft and strange in his mouth. During this sequence, Sabu convincingly conveys first Mowgli's violent ferocity and then his gentle timidity: throughout, he invests this character with an extremely affecting vulnerability.

In *Jungle Book*, we are repeatedly presented with a kind of documentary spectacle of Sabu's impressive abilities at handling real animals in the studio space, but there are also moments when his interaction with the animal characters is produced through judicious editing, and there are also several occasions in which he works with animated or inanimate props. And the dramatic sequence in which Mowgli finally confronts his nemesis, the tiger Shere Khan, is

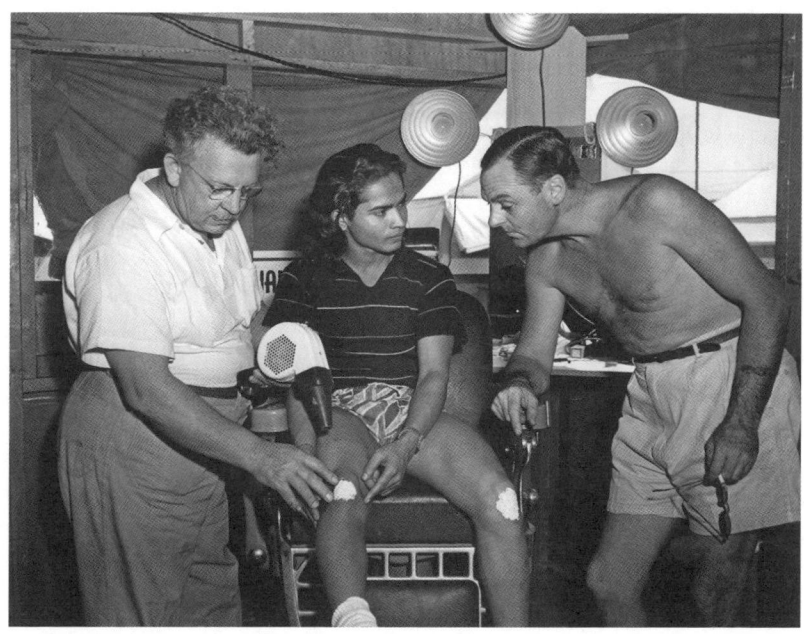

Sabu has his knees dressed while shooting *Jungle Book* (1942)

a particularly powerful example of how Sabu's performance in the film solders together the diverse means deployed by the film to realise Mowgli's relations with the jungle animals for the screen. The sequence begins when the camera pans across a clearing and discovers Mowgli fast asleep, lying on the ground beside the pool in which his buffalo are bathing. Meanwhile, Shere Khan is prowling through the jungle. Various animals sense his presence; an elephant loudly trumpets a warning. Mowgli opens his eyes, lifts his head, and suddenly springs to his feet, aquiver with anticipation: he too can feel Shere Khan nearby. Immediately, Mowgli begins rounding up his buffalo, furiously waving his arms in the air and hollering at the beasts. A long shot shows the animals clambering out of the water and joining the cows that are behind the pool in the background, Sabu as Mowgli in the foreground commandingly conveying them away from danger. Shere Khan is running through the trees towards the village. Mowgli is riding a buffalo in the centre of the herd that is now stampeding through the jungle, waving his staff in the air as the cattle hurtle towards the village. He leaps off his buffalo's back as it gallops through the gates and instantly lunges backwards to help the villagers close the gates. Mowgli is supreme in the midst of this turbulent mayhem, commandeering the scene with incredible authority and magnificent vigour. When Mowgli's mother begs him to seek shelter in the temple with the other villagers, he brandishes his dagger to convince her of his fierce resolve to face the tiger, bounds up some steps onto a roof and begins howling into the jungle beyond the village. 'Don't go,' his mother pleads, 'He will kill you!' Mowgli spins around and declares with a seething scowl: 'No! I shall bring back his yellow hide!' His face is full of fervid intent, and his eyes blaze open as he spits out these words.

Mowgli leaps through a pond, splashing through the waist-deep water and towards the camera before bounding out of view. In the next shot, he tucks up his *lungi* and dives into the river, swimming rapidly (again towards the camera) to where Kaa the snake is coiled upon a gigantic lily pad. Mowgli squats on an adjacent lily pad and begins to ingratiatingly importune Kaa for his assistance. During his interaction with the mechanical prop, Sabu's performance shifts register: his flattering flannel is as phoney as the model snake is fake. With a knowing smile, Mowgli becomes a smarmy snake-charmer, treating Kaa with exaggeratedly deferential obeisance, and for a brief moment Sabu's performance partakes of the Puckish playfulness of Abu the little trickster, as he cajoles the snake into ferrying him downriver and towards Shere Khan.

Mowgli is taunting Shere Khan from the branches of a tree, boldly jeering: 'I won't come down, you come up, to me!'. He throws several rocks at the tiger, and then suddenly Shere Khan jumps up towards where Mowgli stands (rear projection is deployed to suggest this). Visibly frightened by his quarry's strength, Mowgli nevertheless insists 'I'll get your hide today', but these words are uttered much more quietly, as if he had to convince himself anew of his resolve. Sabu's performance thus maintains for the audience an impression of the vulnerability beneath Mowgli's valour. The ensuing sequence comprises shots of Shere Khan prowling about the base of the tree and shots of Mowgli looking down at the tiger from his perch above: Sabu doesn't actually appear in the same shot as the tiger. A rapid succession of close-ups, showing first the actor and then the tiger, both snarling ferociously, functions here to suggest the characters' proximity. Their roars overlap on the soundtrack, so that it is difficult to differentiate the human from the animal. Mowgli's face is ablaze with scorn and fury: 'Come on, *catch* me!' he yells, before grabbing a vine and swinging away. As the tiger follows him on the ground, Mowgli looks over his shoulder, and suddenly smiles, as if now much more certain of his invincibility. The smile suggests Mowgli's exhilaration at his own audacity, and it invites the audience to delight not only in the man-cub's magnificent vigour but also the irrepressible verve with which Sabu here incarnates this character. Mowgli then dives into a river from a promontory, and Shere Khan leaps after him. Next, underwater images show the actor wrestling violently with an obviously stuffed tiger, clasping the prop firmly between his thighs, spinning around and around, before plunging his dagger into the animal's neck. Mowgli lugs Shere Khan's body onto the riverbank, stands up straight and throws back his head and delivers a long mellifluous howl. He then proudly proclaims: 'Shere Khan is dead! I have killed Shere Khan!' and smiles victoriously.

The success of the sequence is dependent upon Sabu's convincing portrayal of his characters' continuous interactions with animals. These interactions are here variously realised for the screen, with the actor required to handle real animals (the water-buffalo) but also talk to and grapple with fake animals (Kaa, Shere Khan), and always with sufficient confidence and conviction for the film's spectacular fantasy to cohere around our sense of and belief in Mowgli's intensely passionate connection with animals. *Jungle Book* undoubtedly capitalises on the star's popular association with exotic animals, established by *Elephant Boy*. The story, moreover, concludes with his character choosing to live with animals rather than his own kind. During the narrative, Mowgli grows increasingly bewildered by the greed and hypocrisy he observes among certain of his human companions: after he prevents the villainous villager Boldeo (Joseph Calleia) from looting the treasure of a nearby lost city, he is falsely accused of murder. Eventually, after saving the entire village from a fire started by the vengeful Boldeo, and disgusted by the destructive violence of man, Mowgli decides to leave the village and resume his life with the animals in the jungle. In the preceding scenes, we have seen him leading the elephants through the burning jungle, and are encouraged to contemplate how much 'the elephant boy' has developed since his first film. No longer perching precariously on his elephant's head (as Toomai had done), Sabu's Mowgli sits with his legs astride the elephant's neck, his shoulders thrown back, his arms resting on his thighs, his muscular torso undulating with the elephant's lumbering gait. He stands beside his elephant when he confronts the villagers for the last time. 'Come back to us' Mowgli's mother calls to her son from the island on which the villagers are sheltering. A medium-close up shows Sabu as Mowgli first cast his eyes down and then slowly look up and almost directly into the camera, just as he had done when he first surveyed the village. Fixing his audience (or

Sabu in Los Angeles in 1942

audiences) with a severe gaze, Mowgli slowly shakes his head from side to side, and says: 'I am of the *jungle* – *their* lair is *my* lair, *their* trail is *my* trail … *their* fight … is *my* fight.' Mowgli then climbs up onto his elephant's head and rides away, upriver, into the jungle. Significantly, Sabu delivers these lines not only with profound solemnity but also with a diminishing force and clarity: the last three words ('is *my* fight') are almost whispered, as if more to himself than to anyone else, as if this is a profound *self-*realisation at the same time that it a public proclamation. The hushed tone with which he concludes this speech suggests the magnitude of his decision: Mowgli refuses the invitation to stay with his human family, and rejects 'culture' and 'civilisation' in order to return to his non-human 'family' – the jungle animals. His destiny, his words suggest, is to *serve* the animals, and to *be led by* the animals in a merging of identities. Ultimately, this is a declaration characterised less by empathy and more by self-effacing humility, as if he identifies *as* an animal, rather than *with* the animals. The 'bestial intensity' of Sabu's Mowgli thus culminates in this powerful scene in which his character rejects human society and professes his allegiance to the non-human. There are, of course, striking parallels with the concluding scene of *The Thief of Bagdad*, in which the 'playground japery' of Sabu's Abu reached its apogee in his character's gleeful rejection of adult society in pursuit of further adventure. In neither film does Sabu's character remain where he is expected to remain, or become what others expect him to become. These conclusions resonate with the way the vigour of Sabu's performances – whether characterised by 'playground japery' or 'bestial intensity' – enabled him to transcend the more objectifying or exoticising tendencies of these films' Technicolor orientalism.

The Thief of Bagdad and Jungle Book consolidated for Sabu two distinct screen personae that remained operative throughout his career, and his roles in these pictures foreshadow the parts he played in his later films. In the oriental fantasies, island adventures and jungle thrillers in which he appeared, Sabu's characters often remain ambiguously or ambivalently positioned in relation to either adult society (if the boyish man-child) or human society (if the jungly man-cub). Just as significantly, moreover, two distinct modes of acting can be discerned in the star's subsequent performances that anchor them to his portrayal of either Abu (and his 'playground japery') or Mowgli (and his 'bestial intensity'). In the roles that refer back to Abu, in films such as *Arabian Nights* (1942) or *Cobra Woman* (1944), Sabu plays the Puckish trickster, the intrepid adventurer, the stalwart sidekick, and he is usually presented in an affectionate bond with an older man. These characters – and Sabu's performances – are effervescent, buoyant, indefatigable, resourceful and infectious. By contrast, in the roles that refer back to Mowgli, in films such as *Song of India* (1949) and *Jaguar*, the characters he plays are more serious, introspective, even melancholy, and often suspicious or critical of human 'civilisation'. While regularly presented in romantic or protective relationships with women (as Mowgli was paired with the village girl, Mahala, played by Patricia O'Rourke), they must reconcile this with their more profound connection to the animal kingdom. In the next two chapters, I turn first to the genre films Sabu made in Hollywood during the war, in which he reprises the 'playground japery' of his Abu with increasingly self-conscious playfulness, and then to the exploitation pictures in which he appeared in the mid-1950s, where the 'bestial intensity' of his Mowgli is resuscitated in order for Sabu to stage a 'comeback'.

Sabu as Orano in *White Savage* (1943)

3: Camp

In the early 1940s, as a contract player for Universal Studios, Sabu appeared in a succession of explicitly escapist genre pictures, including the oriental adventure film, *Arabian Nights*, and two South Sea Island fantasies, *White Savage* (1943) and *Cobra Woman*. The Universal films, which Sabu made during his late teens and early twenties, teamed him up with two other 'exotic' actors, Jon Hall and Maria Montez. The assembly-line productions were essentially vehicles in which the three stars reprised their roles and relationships from film to film: in this 'series', Hall always played the hero, Sabu his faithful and resourceful sidekick, and Montez his romantic interest. These films combine thrilling action, broad comedy and passionate romance: they are resolutely commercial, rampantly populist, strenuously entertaining, and their zany excesses are impeccably ludicrous. This fare proved inordinately popular with American audiences during World War II; critics, however, usually dismissed the films, referring to them as 'spectacular hokum for the masses'.[228] *Cobra Woman*, for example, was described by the *New York Herald Tribune* as 'a costly Technicolor production that turns out to be an unintentionally funny picture', in which '[the] actors are hopelessly lost in a morass of clichés and phony scenes'.[229] The film was acknowledged as demonstrating a 'bravura disregard for the accepted flora, fauna, architecture and anthropology of a South Sea island': it was predicted, rather waspishly, that Universal's next picture would probably feature 'a boxing kangaroo, a polar bear and Bela Lugosi'.[230] Of *White Savage*, one critic suggested that 'the director had assembled odds and ends of properties from *Arabian Nights*, Miss Dorothy Lamour's earlier films and Miss Betty Grable's musical comedies in order to create an exotic environment.'[231] Another critic wryly observed that the studio had by this time (1944) perfected a 'Universal language of lissom legs, thinly-clad breasts and sizzling jungle love-making'.[232] For the studio's efficiently recycled exotica, Sabu's appeal was obvious: as one review noted, *Cobra Woman* once again presented 'the well-formed Maria Montez, with very little on … Jon Hall, who wears more … and Sabu, who wears less'.[233] The star's admirably toned physique, repeatedly displayed in the films, was undoubtedly integral to their erotic (and 'exotic') spectacle: for example, in most of his scenes in *White Savage*, as the island native Orano, Sabu wears only the scantiest of sarongs wrapped around his loins and garlands of pretty white shells draped about his neck. Sabu was famous for being dedicated to personal fitness: in 1944, after he had been living and working in Los Angeles for two years, a feature in *Picture Show* states that

> Sabu works unceasingly to make himself really fit. When he is not working at the studio he is often to be found at the Hollywood Athletic Club, concentrating on swimming, but also having a turn at boxing, wrestling, and gymnastics.[234]

However, the star brings much more to these films than his physical beauty and strength: in these routine romps, Sabu embodies his characters with both rollicking gusto and a larky irony. The impish playfulness of his Abu is here exaggerated, invested with a knowing panache that borders on pantomime, even parody. Cast as the hero's excitable sidekick in one fantasy adventure after another – and functioning, moreover, as an exuberant foil to the tepid, and virtually torpid Hall – Sabu's performances in his Universal films suggest an increasingly self-conscious and self-reflexive handling of the (stereotypical) characters and (stock) narratives supplied for him by the studio. In other words, playing these flimsily drawn (and even more flimsily dressed) characters, Sabu's performances function as camp incarnations.

According to Andrew Ross, camp names an 'exercise' of taste which developed in the 1960s as specific subcultural and elite audiences, 'patrons of the attractive world of immediacy and disposability created by the culture industries in the post-war boom years', redefined notions of cultural capital and asserted new aesthetic sensibilities.[235] Camp, Ross argues, involves a celebrating in the discovery of 'hitherto unexpected value' in the 'obscure or exorbitant object'.[236] In such cases, the 'camp liberator' retrieves 'unsalvageable material' and it becomes 'irradiated … with the glamour of resurrection'.[237] Ross suggests that a 'camp effect' can be created when the films and the stars of 'a much earlier mode of production, which has lost its power to dominate cultural meanings, become available, in the present, for redefinition'.[238] In other words, a camp appreciation of cinema can involve a retrospective resuscitation of the 'disposable' products of a previous era in order to create new meanings and meaningfulness. The 'camp liberator' is engaged in powerful cultural *work* as he 'exercises' his camp sensibility through salvage operations, or appropriations. The value of this kind of work inheres in its extraction of *new* value. Ross argues that camp is 'the *re-creation of surplus value from forgotten forms of labour*'.[239] Camp appreciation involves not only rediscovering 'obscure' objects but remembering the labour that produced those objects in the first place. The labours of the film star thus become 'available for redefinition' through a cinematic 'camp effect'.

The contemporary reviews quoted above suggest how the films were seen as exemplifying an industrial mode of production in which the attractive bodies of popular film stars were presented in overtly conventional (i.e., commercial) exercises. They also demonstrate the delight journalists took in identifying and even ridiculing the films' more ludicrous or exploitative aspects. Such responses anticipate the camp appropriation of these films by gay audiences and queer artists twenty years later. In a recent review of *Cobra Woman*, Genevieve Waller acknowledges that, if considered by traditional aesthetic standards it is a 'terrible' movie, but viewed 'through the lens of camp' the film's various 'shortcomings' produce pleasure for the spectator. Indeed, Waller then argues that *Cobra Woman* is of central significance to camp as a mode of cultural consumption and production precisely because this film actually 'established much of the filmic vocabulary of camp' and 'set the stage for the camp underground cinema to come'.[240] Furthermore, Waller notes that '[for] the majority of his scenes ... [Sabu] is dressed in merely a pair of white shorts, his muscled torso and brown skin on full display and undeniably fetishized', and so because the star is 'seemingly aimed at a gay male and hetero female audience rather than the usual straight male gaze', the film undeniably 'has something to teach us about alternative modes of spectatorship and valuation'.[241] In other words, there would appear to be an explicit relationship between the film's presentation of Sabu as an erotic object for audiences other than straight men and the film's importance for the development of the camp aesthetic. However, homoeroticism has not always been privileged in the camp appropriation of *Cobra Woman*, and thus the film's presentation of Sabu has often been neglected in accounts of the film's significance for the development of the 'filmic vocabulary of camp'. For example, Michael Moon claims that gay male appreciation for these films reveals how gay men growing up in the pre- and Stonewall eras experienced the 'earliest intimations' of their homosexuality as a 'consequence not of noticing [their] own erotic attraction to another boy or man but of enthusiastically enjoying and identifying with the performative excesses of Maria Montez'.[242] Jerry Tartaglia, on the other hand, refers explicitly to Sabu when he argues that the 'veiled homoeroticism' of these films was and remains as important for their reception by gay and queer audiences as the more obviously campy pleasures of the 'languid acting, feeble plots ... and garish but fabulous sets and costumes'.[243]

The popular films in which Sabu starred during the 1940s are of crucial significance to the history of the assertive and idiosyncratic appreciation of popular culture by gay audiences and the subsequent appropriation of that culture by queer artists. The appreciation and appropriation of Sabu's films by gays and queers urges us to consider the significance of non-normative spectatorships and desires for an understanding of Sabu's work in the cinema. Both *The Thief of Bagdad* and the films he made at Universal have been incredibly important in the development of camp, the aesthetic sensibility that is associated chiefly with the reception protocols and artistic practices that some gay men use to assert their homosexual identity and community. This chapter addresses these films in order to examine the relationship between Sabu's presence in the films and their particular appeal for gay male audiences. In a brief summary of the star's career, Priya Jaikumar proposes that, after Sabu moved to the United States in the early 1940s, he became 'something of a gay icon'.[244] I wish to reconsider these films' camp appeal and status in order to address the significance of the star's presence and performances in the films for the history of their appreciation by gay men. Films in which Sabu starred became the inspiration for the artistic practice of two important queer artists in the 1960s: the appropriation of these films by James Bidgood and Jack Smith encourages a re-evaluation of both the film's presentation of Sabu and the actor's performances in the films through the lens of camp. Camp provides a productive and recuperative mode of reassessing Sabu's work as an actor in Hollywood during the war.

The gay underground classic *Pink Narcissus* was made by James Bidgood in his New York apartment between 1964 and 1970. Bidgood's film comprises a succession of vivid homoerotic fantasies and, like Smith's work, was inspired by pictures in which Sabu starred. The film's title, of course, evokes Powell and Pressburger's *Black Narcissus* (1947). Bidgood's film is characterised by an intensely artificial and fantastically ornamental aesthetic: androgynous and effeminate young white men are presented in various stylised and synthetic scenarios, in mauve forest glades, pink and gold boudoirs and opalescent aquamarine lagoons. One sequence in *Pink Narcissus* begins when the protagonist (Bobby Kendall) desultorily spins a globe; he is magically transported to an 'Eastern' palace. A young man, naked but for a gold turban, a gossamer scarf and numerous strings of pearls, dances sinuously and ecstatically for two other men, both of whom are in 'oriental' garb, the younger (Kendall again) wears a spangling turquoise waistcoat and peekaboo harem pants, the older appears in exquisite sultan fancy-dress thrift-store drag. *Pink Narcissus* was Bidgood's eventual response to his seduction when a young boy by the intoxicating colour, exotic imagery and ersatz orientalism of popular films and specifically *The Thief of Bagdad* and *Arabian Nights*.[245] Bidgood's camp sensibility was constituted by the films' fanciful fabrications of foreign lands and ancient times: *Pink Narcissus* represents the fervid fruition of a camp aesthetic which originated with and was inspired by films in which Sabu starred.[246] The camp appropriation of Sabu's films thus also focuses our attention on their homoerotic dimensions, and a queer reading of his characters' situations suggests how they appealed to gay male spectators. In this chapter, the films' display of the star's body will be understood specifically in relation to homoerotic spectacle and gay spectatorship. I am thus interested in how Sabu's films presented his characters in particular kinds of relationship with other men, and with how his characters regarded these men.

At the beginning of *The Thief of Bagdad*, after he has climbed onto the rooftops to evade his pursuers, Abu the little thief played by Sabu is provided with an opportunity to observe King Ahmad. A fanfare announces the presence of the King, and Abu looks down from the rooftops and across to the roof of the palace. The palace would appear to be at some remove from Abu, but the precise distance between the thief and the palace remains ambiguous and indistinct. The film simply cuts back and forth between shots that show Abu leaning forwards and looking down from his rooftop and shots that show the palace from a much closer vantage point. The shots of Abu have clearly been filmed outside: clouds scud slowly across the bright blue sky behind him. The palace, on the other hand, is quite obviously a set inside a studio: a pastel blue sky is painted on a cyclorama in the background. In other words, the sequence comprises shots filmed at different times and in different places which have been edited together to provide the illusion of both temporal continuity and spatial contiguity. The effect is to suggest that Abu and King Ahmad are both *there*, high above Bagdad, at the *same* time. As King Ahmad is announced, he walks slowly and solemnly across the shimmering garnet expanse of the studio floor. Accompanied by the Grand Vizier he climbs some steps that ascend to the very edge of the roof. The film cuts to a medium close-up of his face. He is looking down and to his right, gazing over

Sabu as Kado in *Cobra Woman* (1944)

the city which is presumably visible from the palace rooftop. In the same way that Abu's observation of the palace roof is contrived through editing, Ahmad's surveying of Bagdad is simply implied by the ornate parapet over which the King is shown peering. At this precise moment, the film cuts back to Abu. He is still looking down at the palace roof. Apparently overcome with awe and exhilaration Abu repeats to himself in a hushed voice the words he has just heard: 'Ahmad, the King!' The film then cuts back again to the medium close-up of King Ahmad and, as if he had heard the thief's voice, he looks up with an ambiguous and intensely piercing stare which he fixes at a point just above and directly in front of where he is standing. Rather than provide us with a concluding shot of Abu staring *back* at the King, the image of Ahmad dissolves and we are returned to the scene in the present of the film's narrative in which the King, now a blind beggar, is recounting the various misfortunes that have befallen him.

In his discussion of the film, Jeffrey P. Dennis argues that Abu is presented here as if he were 'falling in love at first sight' with the King.[247] In *The Thief of Bagdad* and *Arabian Nights*, according to Dennis, the moments at which Sabu's characters first encounter the male leads are incontrovertibly suggestive of an intense and erotic attachment.[248] The fierce loyalty and slavish devotion that Sabu's sidekicks display towards the older men functions as an expression of his character's 'unrequited love' for the romantic hero.[249] Abu becomes increasingly frustrated by King Ahmad's relentless desire for the Princess Jasmine. This is particularly the case when he demonstrates his resourcefulness and courage when rescuing the King from danger only for the King to immediately endanger himself (and Abu) all over again in his attempt to protect the Princess from the evil Vizier. At such moments Abu indeed behaves as if he would prefer there was no Princess to come between him and his friend the King. However, the reason I have just described the sequence from *The Thief of Bagdad* in such detail is that I believe it does much more than simply establish Abu's 'homoromantic' regard for Ahmad. The little thief functions in this sequence as a spectator within the film. The pleasure he apparently experiences gazing down at the King from the rooftops is the same as those that are available to spectators as they gaze up at the cinema screen. The fact that the actors' scenes were very obviously filmed at different times and in different places has the result that the thief's erotic regard of the King resembles even more closely the situation of the spectator, since audiences are both spatially and temporally separated from the actors and characters they watch. Observing Ahmad while, at least at first, remaining unobserved *by* Ahmad, Abu functions in this sequence like a member of the audience, 'falling in love at first sight' with the picture's romantic lead. In his subsequent Universal films, Sabu functions to both invite and embody desires that are constitutive of gay male film spectatorship. Not only is Sabu's body objectified so as to appeal to homoerotic desire, but his characters' relationships with the films' male leads not only position the star outside of the films' representation of heterosexual desire but also suggest a distinct realm of homoerotic infatuation. In other words, if the actor's body is in these films offered as an object for a homoerotic gaze, his characters are simultaneously motivated and defined by a similar regard or desire. These films suggest the significance of Sabu for their camp appreciation by gay men because in them he functions not only as an object for homoerotic pleasure at the cinema, but, as an active subject of homoerotic desire in the stories, he becomes a surrogate for the gay male spectator.

Jack Smith, the gay underground film-maker and performance artist, was famously both indebted to and informed by an idiosyncratic regard for the orientalist iconography and exotic opulence of Maria Montez's Universal films.[250] For Smith, *Cobra Woman* was 'the best and worst Hollywood movie ever made'.[251] In 1962, Smith published an essay called 'The Perfect Filmic Appositeness of Maria Montez', a celebration of a 'gaudy array' of 'secret-flix' which privileged Maria Montez's Universal pictures above all others.[252] In the essay, Smith praised their 'stilted, phony imagery', their 'pasty' – meaning artificial or fake – and their 'moldy' – meaning recent but already dated – qualities, and referred to the ersatz exoticism of this 'glittering technicolored trash' as the purest manifestation of cinematic poetry.[253] Smith further evoked this poetry in 'The Memoirs of Maria

Montez or Wait for Me at the Bottom of the Pool,' which is named after a sequence from *White Savage*. For Smith, the beauty and conviction of Montez presented by these films meant that her acting was 'genuine' even though or rather precisely because it was so 'lousy': 'One of her atrocious acting sighs suffused a thousand tons of dead plaster with imaginative life and a truth'.[254] Smith's essays are primarily concerned with evoking the films' sumptuous Technicolor excesses through ironic ekphrasis or remarking on Montez's appearance and performance style. For Smith, the actress's personality was made powerfully palpable in both her strenuous postures and her dementedly and deliriously determined delivery of the film's perfectly inane dialogue. In other words, the visible charisma and endeavour of the actress was, for Smith, as if not more important than the characters she played. Smith's appreciation of these films consists of focusing attention on the way they present as camp spectacle an actor who is visibly hard at work. The camp appropriation of these films by Smith is characterised by a privileging of performance in which new value is extracted from the 'forgotten labours' of the star. Acting should not be visible *as* acting. Camp thus celebrates as a theatrical spectacle the *work* of performance, and is a valuable heuristic for reassessing Sabu's work for Universal.

In his discussion of gay men and Judy Garland, Richard Dyer argues that the camp appreciation of Garland by gay men is partly because there is 'camp in the text of the films themselves'.[255] There are, moreover, important aspects of Garland's performance that contribute to the camp effect: in her gestures and in her delivery of dialogue she 'can be seen to be reflecting back either on her own image in the film or on the vehicle in which she has been placed' and therefore 'mildly sabotaging her roles and films'.[256] Dyer quotes from an article by Wade Jennings, who discerns 'lurking in [Garland's] eyes and the corners of her mouth … [a] suppressed mirth … [that] threatens to mock the silly plot and the two-dimensional character she plays'.[257] Richard Maltby reminds us how

> under the studio system, stars had only a limited amount of power, in no way commensurate with their power to attract audiences at the box-office. Most stars were employed on long, fixed-term contracts with a single studio, and had relatively little control over the roles they were cast in or the movies they made. […] once chosen for a part, however, they could exert some influence over their characterization, and hence over the whole structure of the movies in which they appeared.[258]

Dyer's (and Jennings's) reading of Garland is, I think, instructive and appropriate for a reconsideration of Sabu's performances as a studio 'contract player' in the 1940s films: his labouring in these pictures deserves to be considered as a strategic camping of his public image and screen persona. Paul Robbins, for example, has suggested that Sabu 'had a remarkable ability to convey knowing nods and winks to the audience that let viewers in on his private jokes'.[259] As described by Dyer, camp is 'a characteristically gay way of handling the values, images and products of the dominant culture through irony, exaggeration, trivialisation [and] theatricalisation'.[260] Brett Farmer proposes that camp, as 'a mode of ironic reading', is particularly drawn to star personae which are 'patently excessive in relation to hegemonic definitions of gender and sexuality' and performances which denaturalise 'dominant orchestrations of gender and desire' through a parodying of conventional stereotypes.[261] Similarly, Jack Babuscio suggests that the gay community's enthusiasm for stars whose performances are 'highly charged with exaggerated ... role-playing' functions as a productively oppositional exercise of taste precisely because it asserts and even facilitates an ironic detachment toward the 'restrictive' and repressive roles and identifications which society forces upon both men and women, 'including those on screen'.[262] Camp incarnations of stereotypical characters thus invite audiences to recognise their intrinsic artificiality: camp enables us to perceive in Sabu's performances an operative irony toward the roles he was obliged to play, a *camping* of the image regimes deployed by popular cinema to exploit his 'exotic' appeal.

Arabian Nights

At the beginning of *Arabian Nights*, the crowds of men who have gathered to watch Scheherazade (Montez) dance grow increasingly impatient for the main attraction while the acrobats endeavour to keep them entertained with backflips and somersaults. The climax of the tumblers' act is a spectacular human pyramid during which Sabu's character, the acrobat Ali Ben Ali, performs a headstand balanced on the head of fellow-acrobat Sinbad (Shemp Howard), who is teetering on the shoulders of another member of the troupe. It is while attempting this headstand that Ali Ben Ali first glimpses the noble Haroun Al-Rashid (Hall), who has sought sanctuary on a nearby rooftop after fleeing his enemies. Haroun has become the target of an assassination plot organised by his rebellious brother, the passionate and cruel Kamar (Leif Erikson), who seeks the throne in order to secure the affections of Scheherazade. Ali Ben Ali soon becomes a loyal servant and faithful friend to Haroun. The bond between them is defined chiefly by the acrobat's unflinching admiration for the older man and his eager and enthusiastic assistance in almost any endeavour: their relationship in the film is quite clearly modelled on the relationship between Abu and Ahmad in *The Thief of Bagdad*. And, as if lampooning the scene from the earlier film described above, *Arabian Nights* brings Sabu's and Hall's characters together by presenting a bizarre shot of Ali Ben Ali bent over, his face framed on either side by the backs of his thighs, peering out from beneath his buttocks, first with curiosity, then with increasing consternation, and finally with a grimace of horror as Haroun is felled by an arrow.

During this scene, Sabu's facial expressions are overtly theatrical, exaggerated, and partake of the broad comedy of the dumb-show. Sabu's Ali Ben Ali often behaves in an inordinately acrobatic manner, even when not performing on stage with the rest of troupe, jumping about like a jack-in-the-box whenever he is excited. The star's portrayal of Ali Ben Ali suggests a self-consciously excessive incarnation of his celebrated performance as Abu, the little thief. Indeed, several of the actors appearing alongside Sabu in *Arabian Nights*, such as Shemp Howard (who plays Sinbad), John Qualen (Aladdin) and Billy Gilbert (Scheherazade's manager), were popular comedians, and their performances in the film both draw on their star personae and were intended to remind audiences of their previous screen and stage appearances. For example, Gilbert's celebrated sneezing act, which derived from his work on vaudeville, is incorporated into his performance as the blustering manager. In other words, many of the supporting cast members in *Arabian Nights* contribute to the film's overt and excessive theatricality by both preserving and even parodying the conventional mannerisms and popular routines that were already familiar to audiences. Sabu's performance arguably abides by the same strategy, and thus functions as a self-conscious recycling – and camp theatricalising – of not only his previous screen role as Abu, but also his public image as a perennial man-child.

For example, in one scene Ali Ben Ali must deliver a message to Scheherazade, who has been sequestered inside the harem compound. One of the guards stops him, saying 'Not so fast, little one!' Ali Ben Ali asks the guard whether it is forbidden to enter the harem, and is promptly informed that 'No man but the Caliph' is allowed inside. As Ali, Sabu delivers his lines in an endearingly sweet voice, yet with a sly twinkle gleaming in his eyes. He answers the guard, with excessive incredulity, 'But I'm not a *man*, I'm only a *boy*!' to which the guard replies, 'Boys grow fast! Now be off with you!' Protesting that he is 'only a boy' is

Sabu as Ali Ben Ali in *Arabian Nights* (1942)

simply part of Ali Ben Ali's ploy to gain access to the harem, but Sabu's self-mocking performance invests this encounter with a discernibly ironic tang: after all, the star is quite clearly a grown man rather than an innocent boy. If Universal cast Sabu in *Arabian Nights* in order to capitalise on the star's association with oriental fantasy spectacle – and his role in *The Thief of Bagdad* in particular – his overtly theatrical performance of the part suggests an actor ironically handling the picture's obvious exploitation of his public image.

White Savage

In *White Savage*, we first encounter Sabu when his character Orano dives from a boat into the harbour at Coral Island. Orano's mother, handmaiden to Princess Tahia (Montez) from the nearby Temple Island, asks Orano where he is going. He answers that he must find his 'fellow friend'. Orano means one Kalo (Hall), a fisherman. Kalo wants Tahia's permission to fish for shark in the reefs around Temple Island. As Kalo explains, shark livers are a good source of Vitamin A and a valuable commodity. Throughout the film Kalo affectionately refers to Orano as 'Funny Face', and Orano responds with dutiful obedience. The enthusiastic Orano seems inordinately eager to please Kalo. He is more than merely obliging, he is endearing, ingratiating. He apparently desires only to assist the fisherman, to be his 'little fixer'. When the two meet at Port Coral harbour, Kalo is extremely pleased to see Orano. He holds him firmly by the arms. Orano tells Kalo that Tahia has refused to grant Kalo the fishing rights. A little later Kalo arrives at Temple Island to speak directly with the Princess, unaware that the woman he had met earlier at Port Coral, and to whom he had complained about the Princess, was actually none other than Tahia herself. The Temple Islanders crowd excitedly around Kalo as he comes ashore. Orano dashes energetically through a goat pen and towards the shore, holding a large bouquet of flowers. He welcomes Kalo rapturously. He proceeds to admire the fisherman's clothes: Kalo has dressed in a white suit and straw boater to meet the Princess. Orano remarks on the 'courage' the fisherman has shown by wearing shoes, at which point Kalo gently chucks the smiling Orano on the chin. Orano then demands that the other natives disperse, and shouts 'Go back! This is Orano's friend! Come for a visit! *Good* friend! Even if he does wear shoes!' Then, he hooks his arm in Kalo's and leads him towards the Princess's house. Orano is attentive, protective, possessive. Beneath the palm trees, Orano still holds onto the bouquet of flowers, as if he were too shy to give them to his friend. He instead assures Kalo he will 'fix' things with Tahia, ever eager to do and be what Kalo needs and desires him to be. Orano then finally presents Kalo with the bouquet to give to the Princess, smiling encouragingly, and a little sadly. All goes well between the fisherman and the Princess. The sequence concludes with Kalo locked in a kiss with Tahia, but at that point the camera pans slowly from the couple to where Orano is crouched behind a fence watching them, smiling, and his eyes close in sensuous gratification. He seems to be overcome by a kind of blissful state. Then a guard yanks him away. 'What are you doing?' the guard asks. 'It is what I have *done* that matters!' answers Orano. Unbeknown to Orano, however, the haughty Tahia has already dismissed Kalo: she assumes (perhaps rightly) that he is only interested in the Vitamin A.

Kalo prepares to leave Coral Island, and Orano scampers across the harbour to wish his 'fellow friend' farewell, and presents him with a gift. However, this is in fact a ruse of Orano's to ensure that Kalo stays on the island: the 'gift' in fact belongs to the Princess; Orano has stolen it. Kalo is promptly arrested, and taken by the guards to Tahia's palace the following morning. She is incandescent.

Kalo assumes this must be a joke, and then notices Orano, who is once again observing the couple from a nearby hiding place. When Orano dashes off, Kalo chases him, catches him, and returns to the Princess, pulling the little fixer by the ear. Tahia realises what has happened and begs Kalo's forgiveness, but the fisherman tells her he must speak with Orano alone, and drags him away to an area behind Tahia's throne, grabbing a cane as he goes, as Orano pleads for mercy: 'I didn't mean it! Please don't beat me! Somebody help me!' Princess Tahia winces as she listens to Orano's screams, and we then see Kalo apparently hitting Orano with his cane. Tahia's agitation increases. But the next shot of Kalo pulls back to reveal that he is merely pretending to punish Orano; Orano is in fact perched safely to the side, while Kalo vigorously thwacks the cane on a settle. 'This time you fixed it good!' Kalo stage-whispers, and shakes the cheerful Orano by the hand. As Kalo continues with the subterfuge, Orano yells 'Ow!' again, and then cups his hand around his mouth and promises Kalo he will never lie to the Princess again, proclaiming these words loudly enough for Tahia to hear. Their little improvisation is over: Kalo plants his hand over Orano's 'funny face' and pushes him over onto his haunches; Orano immediately springs back up to spy on his friend's reconciliation with the Princess. The sequence concludes with another close-up of the smiling Orano peeping through the filigree of the throne. He emits a deep sigh of satisfaction as he watches the lovers leave.

This scene presents the homoeroticism between Kalo and Orano as a comic spectacle in which the characters conspire to convince their audience, the Princess, who cannot see them, that things are other than they really are. For a brief while, the audience too is led to believe that Orano is being spanked by Kalo, that Kalo is indeed teaching the 'boy' an important lesson, but then we are let in on their pretence. The delight that both characters display while tricking the Princess in this way effectively connects their sharing of this secret pleasure to the scene of corporal punishment that they are pretending is taking place. Orano, in particular, appears to play his part in this ruse with unnecessary enthusiasm, bouncing up and down on his perch each time Kalo thwacks the settle, as if the imaginary scenario was actually taking place, and as if his bottom was actually reacting to the impact of the cane. As the two characters stage this scene for the purposes of misleading the Princess, the scene in the film functions to suggest how the relationship between Kalo and Orano can be read or understood in two ways at once. There is the gullible Princess, who presumes that what seems to be happening is actually happening, and is thoroughly convinced by the lines of dialogue the men project towards her. The audience, on the other hand knows that something else is happening, and can see that the men are secretly in cahoots. This scene thus solicits gay male spectators both to see through the representation of the relationship between Orano and Kalo that is offered to them, and to imagine that there might be more going on than is ostensibly suggested by the dialogue that the film has its characters speak.

The relationship between Kalo the fisherman and the native 'boy' Orano is thus undoubtedly charged with homoerotic desire, even though or perhaps precisely because Orano must remain absolutely dedicated to helping Kalo achieve *his* desires – initially, the rights to hunt for sharks in Temple Island, and then, eventually, a romantic relationship with the Princess. The relationship between Kalo and the Princess thus functions as an alibi for the fisherman's friendship with Orano, since the pursuit of this romance would seem to require Orano and Kalo to conspire together. In fact, at first, Orano is intent on playing Cupid even before either the fisherman or the Princess have expressed any interest in the other, as if he wanted the relationship to begin precisely for the assistance he could then provide Kalo. At the beginning of the film, the obstacle that stalls the development of the romance between Tahia and Kalo is her suspicion that Kalo is merely pretending to be interested in her so as to persuade her to grant him the fishing rights. Significantly, however, Orano would appear to be unable to imagine that the affection Kalo showers upon *him* is anything but genuine, even though the fisherman's interest in Orano might similarly be explained by the usefulness of Orano's situation in the Princess's household. The fact that Orano *watches* the lovers while smiling and sighing with pleasure means the character functions like the film spectator, but specifically like the spectator who does not desire to pursue the same kind of romantic union, but who can nevertheless enjoy it vicariously in the absence of anything else.

When Kalo is wrongly arrested for the murder of Tahia's brother, Orano refuses to believe that Kalo is guilty but he cannot prove him innocent. Nevertheless, when Kalo is imprisoned it is of course Orano who comes to his rescue, despite the danger involved in helping his friend escape from the lions that are growling and prowling about beneath the precarious wooden platform on which, according to Temple Island custom, Kalo must await his sentence. 'Thanks, funny face!' Kalo says, and he softly punches his 'little fixer' on the chin again. Later, several nefarious types from Coral Island decide to steal the famous precious jewels that are encrusted on the bottom of Princess Tahia's sacred swimming pool. They plan to dynamite the pool in order to get to the hidden treasure. Orano informs Kalo and Tahia what is afoot after seeing the villains arrive on Temple Island. Kalo and Orano then run to the cliff above the cove where the explosives are to be detonated. They dive into the sea and begin swimming towards the ignited dynamite, but they are too late. The subsequent explosion causes the water from the Princess's swimming pool to cascade down over the cliff and directly onto Orano, who sinks to the bottom of the sea, seemingly unconscious. Kalo swims down and drags Orano's body back up to the surface. And then, suddenly, an impromptu earthquake proceeds to destroy much of the temple, and the thieves from Coral Island are killed during the devastation before they have even begun to extract the jewels from the bottom of the pool.

First, then, Orano rescues Kalo from the lions, and then Kalo rescues Orano from the sea. It would appear that Orano and Kalo are always there for each other, and these scenes are among the most dramatic in the film. Kalo never has to rescue Tahia. Nevertheless, the film must of course conclude by privileging Kalo's relationship with the Princess. A little later, Kalo and Tahia are walking beneath some palm trees. They pause on a bridge to embrace. But just before the couple can kiss they are interrupted – by the plaintive bleating of a goat. Nearby, Orano is sitting in a wicker chair, dandling a little goat on his lap, looking over at Kalo and the Princess, and smiling. Kalo and Tahia also smile, and then kiss. The film's final shot shows Orano with his goat. 'See, I fixed it!' he says. As Dennis has observed, in the Universal films heterosexual desire is 'ubiquitous' but the characters played by Sabu express no heterosexual interest of their own.[263] In these films, his sidekicks court the characters played by Hall with an unusually intense aggression, but the object of affection must 'respond with amusement and often affection, but not with longing' because 'his heart belongs' to Maria Montez'.[264] Towards the end of *White Savage*, after Orano has rescued Kalo from the lions, he says to his friend: 'I can always fix things ... *sometimes*.' Orano can and does fix things between Kalo and Tahia. 'Always ... sometimes', however, also suggests sometimes not at all, and one thing that Orano cannot fix is his exclusion from the film's romantic resolution. His position in the film, in other words, is to both facilitate and take pleasure in observing the heterosexual relationship, but once that romance is realised the 'little fixer' becomes superfluous. However, he continues watching, and smiling, even though what he watches would appear not to be available to him, nor even precisely desired by him. Orano remains, then, like the gay spectator, positioned at variance to the heterosexual desire privileged by the film: when he watches his 'fellow friend' passionately smooch with the Princess, he 'fixes' things in the only way available to him – he *stops* watching. Orano closes his eyes, but keeps smiling, as if he were imagining himself in Tahia's place.

Cobra Woman

Cobra Woman, like *White Savage*, takes place on some imaginary South Sea islands. Sabu plays a native islander called Kado. When the film begins, Kado's best friend, Ramu (Hall) is about to marry Tollea (Montez). But before the ceremony can take place, Tollea is taken to the nearby Cobra Island which, she discovers, is ruled over by her twin sister Naja (also played by Montez). Naja is the High Priestess of a cobra-worshipping cult.[265] The unfortunate natives of Cobra Island are routinely sacrificed in order to appease their Cobra King. Tollea's grandmother wants Tollea to help depose Naja and bring peace to the island. Ramu sails to Cobra Island to rescue Tollea, unaware that Kado is hiding in his boat. On the island, Ramu mistakes Naja for Tollea, and both he and Kado are captured. Eventually, Tollea confronts Naja, and Naja falls to her death. The island volcano erupts, destroying the temple. Finally Tollea and Ramu, together with Kado and their chimpanzee friend KoKo sail away from Cobra Island, where democracy has been restored. As usual, it is Sabu's character who appears to be the most capable, the most resourceful and the most dependable during the various escapades on Cobra Island. In the chaos that ensues after the volcano erupts, it is Kado rather than Ramu who manages to kill the Cobra King, although, admittedly, KoKo helps. Kado displays admirable heroism throughout the film, but Sabu's character also functions, again as per usual, to provide erotic spectacle, since he is dressed only in a pair of white shorts while Ramu, in contrast, remains fully clothed. Throughout *Cobra Woman*, Sabu's body is displayed for the audience in scenes in which Kado is repeatedly tied up, stretched out and spread-eagled. While Kado is assuredly courageous, he is also comical, and Sabu speaks here in pidgin English, as do various other islanders but not, significantly, Ramu. And Sabu is also obliged to cavort with the chimpanzee whose name is so similar to his. Sabu once again plays the sidekick, then, and while he appears to be tagging along, he actually saves the day. It is arguably Kado's intense loyalty and devotion to the older Ramu that enables their eventual success. A scene towards the beginning of the film presents Kado's regard for Ramu as particularly appetitive. As the scene continues, and Kado saves Ramu's life, there is the suggestion that Kado's desire for Ramu is so strong that the film requires an animal avatar into which is displaced Kado's homoerotic hunger.

Upon arriving at the Island, Ramu decides to set up camp on the beach for the night. Unbeknown to Ramu, Kado is watching him from further down the coast. Ramu lights a fire, and cooks himself some dinner. Kado is looking on, hungrily licking his lips. Ramu still hasn't noticed him. Then, suddenly, a panther

Sabu as Kado and Jon Hall as Ramu in *Cobra Woman*

slinks stealthily across the rocks above Ramu. Ramu hasn't noticed the panther looming over him, either, but fortunately Kado has. He stands up and reaches for his blowpipe, extends it and blows, killing the panther at the very moment that it leaps down from the rocks. There is the panther, already stiff, or rather *stuffed* (the panther has been replaced by a prop), motionless at Ramu's feet. Ramu is surprised to see Kado, but clearly relieved: 'Am I glad you showed up', he says. Then Kado explains to Ramu that he could see that there was enough food for two, but not for three. In this scene, Kado's gaze would appear to be directed towards the meat that Ramu is cooking on the fire but it is also suggestive of a different kind of hunger or desire, perhaps that Ramu recognise the love which has compelled Kado to follow him to Cobra Island in the first place. However, Ramu is unaware of Kado's presence on the beach and so remains oblivious to the fact that Kado is keeping a patient and protective watch over him. Similarly, he doesn't notice the panther that soon arrives on the scene and which, like Kado, appears to be ravenously hungry. As far as the panther is concerned, Ramu is just as appealing as the meat that he is cooking on the fire, if not more so. The panther's desire for Ramu is thus much more dangerous than Kado's desire but nevertheless appears to be somewhat expressive of it and even continuous with it. The panther provides Kado with an emergency and thus an ideal opportunity to save Ramu's life and be recognised at last, if only for having fortuitously followed Ramu to the island. However, it is as if Kado's desire for Ramu *summoned* the panther precisely so that he could enact his desire for Ramu in a way that his friend could actually acknowledge. Luckily for Ramu, Kado has his extendable blowpipe to hand.

In *Jungle Book*, released the previous year, the man-cub Mowgli is believed to possess strange shape-shifting powers, specifically the ability to transform himself into a panther. In one scene, he and his panther friend Bagheera conspire to convince a villager that Mowgli can indeed assume the shape of a panther. (Indeed, in *Jaguar*, a later film, Sabu's character fears he may be cursed with just such a shape-shifting propensity.) If the panther in *Cobra Woman* represents those desires that Kado has for Ramu that cannot otherwise be expressed, it absolutely must be killed, as those desires must be controlled and stilled. The dead panther that flops onto the beach, however, is patently a fake panther, and is obviously a prop standing in for the real living panther used in the previous shots. The stilling of Kado's desire for Ramu that is apparently achieved by the killing of the dangerous panther into which that desire had been displaced is, then, in the end unconvincing. Kado's desire has been quelled but not exactly quenched.

At the end of *Cobra Woman*, Ramu and Kado are sailing away from Cobra Island. KoKo accompanies them. Suddenly, Tollea appears – she has decided to leave her island to be with Ramu. The couple kiss, passionately, but are then immediately distracted by KoKo, who honks from the other side of the boat. Sabu, as Kado, is leaning over the rear of the boat, shot so that his own rear end is prominently displayed. It would appear that the adventures on Cobra Island have finally taken their toll on Kado's little white shorts, for KoKo is busy with a needle and thread, apparently repairing a tear in the shorts. Ramu and Tollea laugh, of course. The next shot moves us much nearer to where KoKo is mending Kado's shorts and offers us a closer view not only of the backs of Sabu's thighs but also of the actor's right buttock, which is revealed by the rip in the white fabric. Ramu and Tollea laugh again: 'The End'. The film thus concludes, like *White Savage*, with an image of the heterosexual couple's embrace interrupted by the comic spectacle of Sabu's character coupled with an animal. In the earlier film, you will recall, it was a little goat, now it is the chimpanzee. However, the end of *Cobra Woman*, by focusing our attention in this way on Sabu's rear end and offering such a ridiculous image of the actor's exposed behind, is arguably parodying the convention by which his characters are excluded from the films' romantic resolutions precisely because they must remain exclusively devoted to, and openly available to, the needs and desires of the male leads. In other words, the 'homoromantic' relationship between Sabu's and Hall's characters, which recurs across the three films in which the actors were paired by the studio, both begins and ends with somewhat ludicrous scenes in which the films intentionally draw our attention to Sabu's behind.

While the near-constant display of Sabu's half-naked body in these films offers the actor to gay male audiences as an object of erotic contemplation, the actor also plays characters whose relations with other men provide opportunities for recognising the desire of the gay male subject. And because this desire cannot be reciprocated in the films themselves, it closely resembles the spectators' desires for the stars whose images appear on the screen, including, of course, Sabu himself. The star's characters always function in these films as invested but ultimately excluded onlookers of the heterosexual desire that organises the representation of his co-stars' characters. They are exempt from the inevitable romantic resolutions with which the films must conclude, and so remain available and amenable as surrogate subjects for the gay male spectator's experience of the films themselves.

In these Universal films, moreover, not only do Sabu's characters partake of his familiar Puckish trickster persona, but, more significantly, so do his performances, as if the star were approaching his roles with the same tactical verve that Abu demonstrated when he expertly inveigled honey for his pancake, or that Mowgli showed when he artfully importuned Kaa for his assistance. In his previous two films, as their top-billed star in the leading role, Sabu transcended their Technicolor spectacle with the dynamic vitality of his performances. Cast as a sprightly sidekick in his Hollywood pictures, the star becomes a supplementary figure, but in this capacity he serves to garnish this preposterous and outrageous tosh with a pronouncedly zingy felicity. Indeed, as his characters in the series become more caricatured, so his acting style becomes even more buffoonish, encouraging us to view his excessively theatricalised performances as self-consciously zesty 'citations' of his established image, as a slyly strategic camping of his popular identity. Increasingly utilised as exotic cheesecake in the South Sea island adventure fantasies that followed quickly on the heels of *Arabian Nights*, the smirky pizazz of Sabu's performances nevertheless suggest not only his professional *savoir vivre* but also that, as Dyer argued of Garland's self-consciously camp gestures, the star 'can be seen to be reflecting back either on [his] own image in the film or on the vehicle in which [he] has been placed'.[266] As such, Sabu's performances in the Universal films might be understood in relation to what José Muñoz has called *disidentification*, a 'mode of dealing with dominant ideology' in which a marginalised subject 'tactically and simultaneously works *on*, *with, and against* a cultural form'.[267]

4: Trash

Sabu is most often remembered for either the films he made with Alexander Korda during the late 1930s and early 1940s, or for the films he made for Universal Studios after he moved to Hollywood. After the end of World War II, and after his contract with Universal came to an end, Sabu continued to find sporadic work as a screen actor, but the kinds of films for which he was famous were no longer being made, and the films in which he did appear were of an altogether different category to those he had made previously. They were certainly produced for much less money than the star's earlier films, and were therefore made much more quickly, and sometimes very rapidly indeed. Sabu worked with independent producers such as Monty Schaff and Albert S. Rogell on several such films in Hollywood during the late 1940s and then, upon his return to Hollywood in the mid-1950s, the star made several attempts to break into television, while still performing leading roles in low-budget 'quickies'.

Sabu's films and television work during this period were organised around the commercial exploitation of their star's waning popular appeal. After *Black Narcissus*, Sabu's films usually presented him as a heterosexual protagonist whose romance or relationships with women were central to the narrative, in stark contrast to the sidekick roles he had in the Universal films. Promotion for these later films sought to exploit the films themselves, by proclaiming the pleasures they provided in crude and hyperbolic fashion, and also their intended audiences, by appealing to their desires for 'cheap' sensation, thrills and spectacle. Indeed, 'exploitation' originally referred to the marketing strategies used to advertise such films. For instance, a poster produced for *Man-Eater of Kumaon* presents an image of a tiger the size of a double-decker bus looming over a half-naked Sabu and his love interest, played by Joanne Page. 'Never Before Have You Lived An Adventure Like This!' the poster says. 'Drama Screams With Excitement When Jungle Beast Stalks His Beautiful Victim!' Similarly, a poster for *Song of India* declares: 'Indian Kingdom Rocked! Prince Duels Pauper For Royal Love! Claw

And Fang Against Knife And Bullet! A Woman's Wiles Against The Jungle's Curse!' (It was while making *Song of India* for Rogell in 1948 that Sabu met Marilyn Cooper, who was working on the film as Sabu's co-star Gail Russell's stand-in; the couple were married in October. They had two children, Paul, born 2 January 1951, and Jasmine, born 22 March 1958). These films were, on the whole, derivative genre pictures, mixing romance and danger in either jungle or tropical settings, and were obviously intended to exploit their star's popular associations with wild and exotic animals and incredible adventure.

Since the star is an actor or entertainer whose popularity and appeal depend upon a specific image constructed by and maintained through performances, publicity and the media, the star can, in certain circumstances, exploit his own image in order either to maintain his professional profile or simply continue his career. In the early 1950s, Sabu seized various opportunities to exploit and therefore capitalise on his popular associations with both the 'the Orient' and, of course, elephants. For instance, on Valentine's Day in 1951, Sabu reprised his *Thief of Bagdad* persona when he starred in a lavish 'musical comedy on ice' extravaganza called *Thief of Ice-Arabia* at the re-opening of Earl Carroll's Million-Dollar Theatre Restaurant.[268] (Sabu had been an avid ice-skater since he was a young boy; he sometimes told journalists that he wanted to be a professional ice-skater should he stop working for the cinema.[269] He had also expressed an interest in combining these pursuits by making a film with Sonja Henie, the Norwegian Olympic ice-skater who featured in a series of musicals during the late 1930s.)[270] More importantly, perhaps, the star spent several years working as a circus performer in Europe. Sabu appeared with a troupe of trained elephants as one of the attractions at Tom Arnold's Christmas Circus in Harringay Arena in London during the Christmas season of 1951. According to a review in *The Times*, Sabu's elephants '[performed] feats of balance and judgment unexpected in large animals ... but in skill and agility Miss Edith Crocker's bears that ride bicycles and Mr. Franz Althoff's Alsatian dogs that ride a pony are equally impressive'.[271] It was while touring Italy with a circus in 1952 that Sabu returned to the cinema and played an Indian prince in *Buongiorno, Elefante!* (eventually released in England with the title *Hello, Elephant!* and in the United States as *Pardon My Trunk*), which co-starred Vittorio de Sica as a school teacher who, after assisting the Prince, is rewarded with a baby elephant. In other words, Sabu's various performances during this period, whether they were on an ice rink,

Sabu as 'Sabu' in *Sabu and the Magic Ring* (1957)

in the circus ring or for a film, were clearly characterised by an exploitation of the audiences' memories of and fondness for the star's performances in his earlier films. At the same time, of course, these performances presented Sabu with the opportunity to exploit certain of his own skills, such as his confidence with animals, his prowess as an ice-skater, and, of course, his abilities as an actor, even as they obliged him to participate in and therefore perpetuate those associations (between Sabu and the Orient, between Sabu and elephants) which had always constituted his star image and which would always thus determine the kind of work he was offered.

The 'sexual scandal,' according to Richard deCordova, 'is the primal scene of all star discourse, the only scenario that offers the promise of a full and satisfying disclosure of the star's identity.'[272] While touring with the circuses in Europe, Sabu's personal affairs became the focus of media attention. In the spring of 1949, Sabu was charged in a paternity action by a ballet dancer whom the star had met while making *Black Narcissus* in England in 1947. The dancer, Brenda Marian Julier, claimed that Sabu was the father of her daughter, Michaela, who had been born in Dublin, Ireland, in September 1948, a month before Sabu and Marilyn Cooper were married. On 24 May, an article in the *Los Angeles Times* published details of the dancer's 'Romance with Former Elephant Boy of Films': it reported that Julier's petition demanded the star provide $500 a month to support the child, and added that 'the complaint [asserted] that Sabu [had] accumulated a fortune of more than $350,000 and [received] about $50,000 a year for his film work'. According to Frank Catlin, Julier's attorney, the dancer and the film star were engaged in the summer of 1947, and she had stayed with Sabu in America for six months, after which the engagement was broken off and Julier returned to England. The article concluded that both Julier and her daughter were expected to come to Los Angeles in June for the preliminary hearing.[273] However, it was not until October the following year that the case reached the courts, by which time Julier was married to Frank Ernst. On 9 October, according to newspaper reports, Julier testified in court that the she had 'lived in Sabu's room' and had told the star she was pregnant while they were staying in a hotel in Del Mar, California. She claimed that she had then been sent back to England and that her letters to Sabu received no replies.[274] The *Los Angeles Times* continued its coverage of the trial, and reported on the questioning of Julier by Sabu's counsel, Sydney R. Williams, on 14 October, under the headline 'Dancer at Sabu Trial Denies Affair in Egypt'. During cross-examination, the article states, it was put to Julier that she had both described 'a love affair with a gentleman in Egypt' in a letter to a friend (to which she had replied, 'I did not') and that she had 'shared a motel room with Sabu's brother, Shaik, and another man, Mark Klenner, in August 1947', at which point 'Mrs. Ernst shouted: "It is not true."'[275] The newspaper article also stated:

> Sabu, through Williams, claims he is not the father, has never been intimate with Mrs. Ernst, and that he brought her to this country to 'be nice to her' in order to avoid threatened publicity which 'would kill him in pictures'.[276]

On 17 October, it was reported in one newspaper that 'Sabu, 26, the elephant boy of the films, sent judge and jury into uproars of laughter … with his explanations that he couldn't be in the company of women while he was making pictures with wild animals.'[277] In a story with the headline 'Tigers, Women, and Love Won't Mix, Sabu Says', the star's responses to Catlin's questions were quoted at length. The article claimed that Sabu had told the court that in the summer of 1947 he 'was making a picture with wild animals … and for [his] own protection had to avoid contact with women': 'He added that love making would arouse the animals' "ferocity and desire to kill".'[278] The article added 'Sabu also said that because of a back injury he suffered in London in February, 1947, lovemaking would not have been a comfortable pastime for him.'[279] As another headline put it: 'Sabu, on Stand, Denies Being Father of Child: Actor Reiterates under Oath That He Never Made Love to English Dancer Suing Him.'[280] On 19 October, it was reported in the *Los Angeles Times* that the jury had cleared Sabu.[281] In Williams's closing address, the newspaper stated, he referred to the actor as 'a sweet, lovable boy, wide open for a suit of this kind', and that Sabu was unaware of the child's existence until the paternity suit was filed, adding: 'He is not an ordinary motion picture star. He is not an ordinary person. Animals love him. People love him.'[282]

As Adrienne L. McLean has suggested, scandals are 'always discursive constructions as well as events'.[283] The newspapers' coverage of the trial focused readers' attention on/exploited the public's awareness of the long-standing and popular ideas about Sabu's uncanny understanding of and affinity with wild and dangerous animals. The articles quote the star's attorney's description of Sabu, in which he suggests the defendant is 'not … ordinary', or, in other words, unusual, and exceptional, precisely due to his mysterious abilities with animals, who, it is claimed, 'love him'. The apparently incredible confidence and courage that the star reportedly routinely displayed when working with such animals on the set becomes during the trial absolutely central to the star's defence. Knowledge of and interest in his public and professional life as the star of jungle pictures are thus exploited during the representation of the star's private and personal life in the defence. Furthermore, his performance in court, according to the coverage, provided entertainment for those in attendance, as his private affairs were made a matter of public record and the focus of media attention. Furthermore, the coverage suggests that Sabu protected his reputation in court by explaining how he protected himself while working with animals on his films. Sabu tells Catlin that sexual abstinence is the 'secret' method he deployed in order to work safely with animals: 'That's why I can get in the cage with the tigers', he is quoted explaining.[284] The revelation (and the subsequent reporting) of this 'secret' thus exploits the public's fascination with Sabu's exceptional affinities with animals by asserting that the star's sex life is organised around his professional obligations, and that his work, the basis of his public profile and popular appeal, takes precedence over his personal affairs.[285]

Sabu travelled to India in the autumn of 1953 and stayed until the spring of 1954. He arrived with his wife and their young son, Paul. The *Times of India* referred to the star as 'Sabu Dastagir, the Indian boy who leapt to fame in the Hollywood film, *The Elephant Boy* [sic]', and then noted approvingly that he had 'returned to his motherland after a lapse of 17 years'. The article reports that Sabu had 'entered into a contract with Kishore Sahu to play the leading role in his forthcoming picture, *Sauda*'.[286] (According to Gayatri Chatterjee, during Sabu's trip to India he was sought to play a leading role alongside Nargis in the Mehboob Khan production that would become *Mother India* (1957); the part intended for Sabu, Birju, eventually went to Sunil Dutt, who then married Nargis).[287] Another story in the same newspaper, published a few days later, suggested that Sabu had for a long time been 'keen to visit the land of his forefathers', adding that 'it is uncharitable to say, as has been suggested, that Sabu has returned to India primarily to star in a film'. When Sabu met Kishore Sahu in Europe, the article explains, the trip to India had already been planned.[288] In other words, the reason for Sabu's arrival in India became a matter of public debate. While the coverage in the *Times of India* presents the star's visit as if he were a prodigal son, returning to his homeland, it nevertheless acknowledges that the actor had been accused of being compelled less by patriotic or nostalgic feelings than by professional, and therefore financial considerations. In other words, Sabu was both welcomed 'home' by fans, but also treated with circumspection by those who doubted his motivations. After Sabu had begun working on the production for Kishore Sahu, a series of articles and several cartoons that were printed in the English-language film magazine *Filmindia* represented the star in ways that expressed and exploited 'uncharitable' opinions of Sabu similar to those that the *Times of India* had attempted to squelch. In the late 1930s, Sabu was severely criticised in *Filmindia* by its editor Baburao Patel for his participation in *The Drum*, and the magazine had accelerated its campaign against the 'anti-Indian' films being produced in Europe and the United States after that film's release in India had led to rioting in several cities. In other words, the magazine had earlier identified the star as having betrayed his Indian 'forefathers', and denigrating the 'motherland', by appearing in Korda's imperial cinema. In 1954, however, the magazine was more interested in Sabu's status as a Hollywood star, and his personal affairs, than it was concerned with castigating the star for his associations with pro-colonial films like *The Drum*.

Throughout the spring of 1954, *Sauda*, the Sahu production in which Sabu was to star, was promoted on the pages of *Filmindia*. Posters for the film appeared in the February, March and April editions of the magazine, describing it as 'A Saga of Love and Hate – On the Palm-fringed Malabar Coast – Beside a Sunny Sea!' Sabu's co-stars in *Sauda* were Shashikala Jawalker-Saigal, known simply as Shashikala, and Roopa Verman, both of whom were popular young actresses at the time. In the April edition an article about Sabu's behaviour inaugurated the trashing of Sabu that the magazine then sustained until the star's departure later that year. The magazine ridiculed his 'elephant boy' persona, as well as his love of automobiles and his association with Hollywood jungle pictures. For example, a tidbit in the magazine's regular 'Bombay Calling' feature refers to 'the strenuous efforts made by Sabu, our Elephant Boy, to be noticed by his countrymen as a great film star from Hollywood'. The article reports that

[having] moved unnoticed for days through streets and studios, the elephant boy took out his streamlined American car on the roads. And lo, the miracle happened! That car brought out the question: 'Who's [sic] car is that?' And Sabu gave the silly Sahu smile – the one with which Chembur is lighted up. [Chembur is a neighbourhood in Mumbai.][289]

With this pot-shot, *Filmindia* ridicules the star's behaviour, and represents him as a vain and disingenuous clown. The 'silly … smile' that is attributed to Sabu refers the magazine's readers to the star's celebrated smile, which was the focus of so much attention in the British media when he had first become a star almost twenty years earlier. The reference to Sabu using his American car to attract the crowds' attention suggests that the magazine sought to emphasise his relationship to America, and exploit its readers' knowledge of his life in the United States, as a way to impugn the star's behaviour during his stay in India.

Scurrilous features and satirical cartoons appeared in *Filmindia* that exploited the readers' interest in the Hollywood star by proffering insinuations about his relationships with his female co-stars in the film. In the March edition, it was reported that one month of outdoor shooting for *Sauda* had been completed, including various scenes filmed in the Chalakudi forests, 'sixty miles from civilization': 'Sabu, the elephant boy', the article observed, 'seemed to be at home amongst the elephants.'[290] *Filmindia* began printing photographs of Sabu and his co-star Shashikala in the same issue. In one such photograph, Sabu is shown bare-chested, Shashikala holds on to him in a melodramatic pose. The image is captioned: 'Sabu, the well-known Hollywood actor, makes his first Indian romantic team with Shashikala, our popular starlet, in *Sauda*, a sensational romance.'[291] In the months that followed, *Filmindia* sought to insinuate that there was more to this 'romantic team' than the 'sensational romance' in which they were both starring. In April's issue a photograph of Shashikala is captioned: 'See how Shashikala attracts Sabu's attention in *Sauda* … .'[292] In the May issue a photograph of Sabu resting his head on Shashikala's knees is captioned: 'That is a new one Shashikala has adopted. His name is Sabu and he gives her some Hollywood thrills in *Sauda*, a jungle romance … .'[293] These photographs all show the actor and actress in their characters' costumes, in poses that suggest their characters' relationship in the film, but are repeatedly deployed in order to make insinuations about the stars' off-screen relationship. One such photograph is captioned: 'Shashikala seems to have arrived at the cross-roads of destiny while meeting Sabu in *Sauda*, a romantic tale … . Let us hope she sticks to the old, well-trodden path.'[294] Beneath another photograph of the stars working on the shoot is printed: '"Come to Hollywood", says Sabu to Shashikala. She sees the vision and seems to like it.'[295] Shashikala was at this time a wife and mother, having married a businessman, Om Prakash Saigal, when she was 18, several years earlier. Sabu's wife had initially accompanied the star in India the previous year, but had now returned home. In the same issue the 'Bombay Calling' feature included a more pointedly suggestive reference to Sabu's relationships with the actresses who starred with him in the film:

[With] Mrs. Marilyn Sabu sent back to America, Hollywood's elephant-brand film actor Sabu is reported to have given some soap treatment to film actress Shashikala in a brave effort to wash off the ghee which she picked up from Hubby

Om Prakash Gheewalla ... Shashikala is not looking greasy any more and is likely to fly to Hollywood for a role in a jungle picture. Elephants and elephant boys seem to be great ones at lifting people from obscurity ...Nimmi, that vest-pocket virgin with unkissed lips, also wanted elephant boy Sabu to teach her how to ride an elephant. Sabu did put her on the trun and heaved her up but in doing so Nimmi bumped into Shashikala who was already up there. After that Sabu ran for his life and the elephant got mad.[296]

On the same page, there is a cartoon to illustrate the story, which depicts the two actresses fighting each other on top of an elephant, which chases after Sabu. Shashikala is saying 'You can't have two on one elephant', to which Nimmi replies 'Why not? I came up the same trunk.' The elephant exclaims 'Eh, Sabu, they are scratching my back', and Sabu answers: 'Sorry, Pal – But I can't risk a scratch.'[297] (*Filmindia*'s reference to Sabu's 'treatment' of Shashikala plays with the meaning of the word 'sabu' – soap). The following month, the magazine praised Shashikala for having 'suddenly become husband-conscious', and observed: 'The foreign "soap" seems to have failed in washing off the local "ghee" from this domesticated little woman'. On the same page, a cartoon shows Sabu boarding a plane. Shashikala waves him off, while Sahu weeps to one side.[298] Sabu indeed departed India, and *Sauda* was never completed.

The film and television projects that Sabu worked on after his return to the United States are generally regarded in relation to exploitation or 'trash'. In these films, Sabu's labours become organised around an exploitation of his screen persona that amounts to a 'trashing' of that image. These later films are difficult to see today, for only a very few are commercially available on DVD, and rarely, if ever, have they been considered worthy of serious critical consideration. These are the films that are routinely mentioned, but then summarily dismissed, whenever reference is made to the star's decline in popularity following World War II, and are usually described as undistinguished, formulaic, commonplace, mediocre or worthless. If they are remembered at all, it is principally due to Sabu's involvement, and they are cited as evidence of the star's having become, while still in his late twenties and early thirties, a 'has-been', reduced to appearing in increasingly ropy run-of-the-mill productions. These films are, however, significant for a re-evaluation of the trajectory of Sabu's career as an actor in the postwar period because they reveal his attempts to maintain a public profile by appearing in increasingly exploitative material. Moreover, they are important for an understanding of the contemporary circulation of his star image because these films have recently been recuperated (though not necessarily *redeemed*) by what Jeffrey Sconce has described as the 'neo-camp aesthetic' of a 'deviant taste public', 'infatuated with the artifice and excess of obsolescent cinema', and dedicated – even devoted – to 'cultural detritus', including 'all forms of cinematic "trash"'.[299]

The has-been is a particular category of star, one whose fame outlasts their market value, who is suspected of being past their prime. The has-been thus remains a public figure despite the fact that his popularity with audiences, and therefore his appeal for commercial producers, is widely perceived to be incontrovertibly, but not necessarily irrevocably, in decline. The labours of the has-been are typically organised so as to effect a 'comeback', to revitalise his career, and thus to resurrect his former and more profitable presence in the industry. For this reason, the comeback usually attempts to reactivate public interest in the star, specifically by exploiting audiences' memories of his earlier films, and by extracting as much meaning and value as possible from the recognisability of the star's name, face and body. In the exploitation film, which Paul Watson has described as 'a blatantly commercial product … designed to ensure maximum possible return from the minimum investment and resources', the has-been functions not only to keep the costs down (since they can no longer demand high salaries) but also – if all goes well – to increase profits (because of the public's familiarity with their popular image).[300] The exploitation of the image of the star, whether by that star or by his employers, must always involve the labour of the actor working to approximate that image, to re-activate it, and to re-animate it. Public awareness of the incredible story of Sabu's childhood in the jungles of India is taken for granted by films that purport to examine the violent 'nature' of 'savages'. Popular memory of the star's earlier roles in films like *Elephant Boy* and *Jungle Book* is deliberately evoked by the insipid jungle thrillers and serials in which Sabu was repeatedly cast as a 'jungle boy'. It is in such film and television work that we can perhaps most clearly see the exploitation of Sabu's popular image. Of one such film, *Jaguar*, the critic for *Variety* wrote: 'This routine yarn about murderous jaguar-men in the Amazon jungle has the sole advantage of Sabu's name for the less discriminating program market'.[301] The attempt to resuscitate the star as a viable commodity becomes discernible in the sheer professionalism – the unflagging assuredness – of the actor's performances, in which it is difficult to distinguish between the actor's admirable commitment to the comeback (or their career) and their characters' indefatigable conviction within the various situations that constitute the film's attempts to thrill. As actors are perceived mustering the energy necessary to maintain the fiction, the blatant effort of their performances can produce an alienation effect. As Gary Hentzi has suggested, in 'low-budget movies, turned out by a kind of film industry underclass, who pride themselves on their ability to do without' – genre pictures which undoubtedly deserve their status as 'schlock' – audiences become particularly conscious of the actors involved, as 'the thin artifice of character, setting, and incident becomes vitalized by our awareness of the real people behind it'.[302] In other words, the more threadbare the production, and the more inadequate the resources, then the more essential – and more visible – become the star's labours as a performer.

Jaguar

In the summer of 1954, Sabu collaborated with Mickey Rooney on a number of film and television products. In July, the trade journal *Billboard* announced that Mickey Rooney Enterprises was planning to make three television series, including *The Magic Lamp*, which would star Sabu.[303] A fortnight later, *Billboard* reported that financing for *The Magic Lamp* had been concluded, and that shooting of the pilot episodes would begin the following September. The show is described as 'a fantasy for children, based on stories such as *The Arabian Nights*, complete with flying carpets and genii'; the pilots would be produced 'coincident with the filming of a Mickey Rooney Enterprises theatrical release, *Jaguar*, in cooperation with Republic Pictures'.[304] Republic Pictures was an independent corporation which both produced and distributed low-budget genre pictures and serials, Westerns in particular. Established in 1935, when six Poverty Row outfits were consolidated by one of their investors, Republic Pictures was eventually responsible for several successful films during the early 1950s, such as *Rio Grande* and *The Quiet Man*, both directed by John Ford and starring John Wayne, and *Johnny Guitar*, directed by Nicholas Ray, but by the middle of the decade the company was in rapid decline, and in 1958, production ceased, with distribution ending the following year. Both *Jaguar* and *The Magic Lamp* pilots were to be directed by George Blair, and produced by Maurice Duke. However, the pilot episodes of Sabu's television series failed to attract national sponsorship, and so no more episodes were made. Several years later, the two pilot episodes of *The Magic Lamp* were edited together and released in theatres with the new title *Sabu and the Magic Ring* (1957). The television series had intended to exploit the waning appeal of the star by combining diverse elements of his most successful films, specifically *The Thief of Bagdad* and *Arabian Nights*. The show was set in

Press book for *Jaguar* (1956)

Uzbekistan, and focused on the adventures of a stable boy, played by and also named Sabu, and his elephant. Posters for *Sabu and the Magic Ring* duly advertised the film by proclaiming it presented 'The Amazing Adventures of Sabu, the Elephant Boy of Samarkand', and promised audiences no fewer than '1001 Monstrous Thrills!' Sabu's mid-1950s comeback thus deliberately sought to capitalise on the screen personae and acting styles associated with his most successful films: if for *The Magic Lamp* Sabu was obliged to revive the 'playground japery' of his portrayal of Abu, for *Jaguar* he was required to reprise the 'bestial intensity' of his performance as Mowgli.

The film takes place in South America. Sabu plays 'Juano', born to an obscure Amazonian tribe widely rumoured to be murderous jaguar-worshipping savages. Juano was 'discovered' in the jungle when he was a very young boy by an ethnologist, Doctor Powell (Jonathan Hale), who then decided to raise the boy as if he were his son. Now, fifteen years later, Juano is preparing to go to university to study ethnology and join his 'father' in the field. Powell, meanwhile, agrees to join a jungle expedition led by two oil prospectors, Steve Bailey (Barton MacLane) and Marty Lang (Touch Connors). Bailey asks the doctor about Juano, after hearing the incredible story of the Doctor's 'son'. 'He's as civilised as you or I', Powell assures them. 'Where do you keep him locked up?' Bailey then asks. Powell smiles, and calls for Juano. Sabu enters the room, very smartly dressed in a short-sleeved shirt, long trousers, with Brilliantine glistening in his hair and, somewhat anomalously, a long wooden spear in his hand. He greets his adoptive father's guests cordially, but they refuse to shake his hand, eyeing him with suspicion. Juano then briefly discusses the spear with the doctor: it belongs to Powell's collection of tribal artefacts. When Juano leaves, Bailey says to the doctor, 'Hard to believe that only fifteen years ago he was just a little savage.' Rita (Chiquita), Powell's secretary – and Juano's girlfriend – arrives to find Juano upset: 'They stared at me as if I were some sort of a wild animal,' he says. Later, at the dock, Bailey fights with one of the Indians loading crates onto the boat, and ends up in the river. Juano and Doctor Powell are there, and Juano grabs a spear. 'Don't Johnny!' cries Doctor Powell (he often calls Juano 'Johnny'). But then he realises that Juano was aiming at the crocodile swimming towards the floundering Bailey. 'For a moment I thought ...' Doctor Powell mumbles. Even the doctor, it would appear, doubts that his 'son' has been fully 'civilised'. Suddenly, piranha fish begin devouring the crocodile, and Juano rushes to the dockside to help Bailey. Shortly after, Juano joins the expedition, because a letter from the university insists that the quota is full.

'There is no place in the university for savages!' Juano spits, angrily smashing a pot to the floor.

During the expedition, several characters are killed. All the evidence suggests the jaguar-worshipping tribesmen are responsible. We have seen them from time to time, scurrying around in the jungle, dressed in what look like jaguar-print romper-suits. Unfortunately Juano comes under suspicion, too, and only Rita and Doctor Powell believe in his innocence. Then Powell is killed, and Juano becomes convinced that he must have murdered his 'father' while in some kind of crazed jaguar trance. Juano decides to 'return' to the tribe: the film shows Sabu, running through the jungle set, desperate with confusion and exhaustion, without his shirt, his trousers suddenly ripped to shreds, and with his hair hanging down over his face. Juano stops at a small jungle pool for a drink, failing to notice the gigantic snake spooled about the branches of the tree above his head. He crouches down, drinks, and splashes water on his face, while the snake slowly unravels itself and descends towards him. Distinctive markings on the snake's skin suggest it is a boa constrictor. Then Juano stands up, and headbutts the snake, and then, someone else altogether – a stuntman, it would appear – is struggling with the boa constrictor. Two tribesmen are watching from nearby. The stuntman spins around, effectively winding the snake about his own body. The two tribesmen continue watching. The snake is coiled tightly about the stuntman's waist, shoulders and face, and he staggers about, his back to the camera. Then, the film cuts to a shot of Sabu, standing with a huge rubber snake wrapped around his shoulders, and it now lacks markings of any kind. Gripping the rubber snake's head with his left hand, Juano pulls out his knife. The film cuts to show the stuntman once more, also wielding a knife, but then collapsing onto the ground. One of the tribesmen takes aim with a bow and arrow. Meanwhile Sabu, still standing up, is still holding the head of the rubber snake with both his hands. The tribesman's arrow pierces the rubber snake's head, and Juano shimmies free, panting with relief.

During this sequence, *Jaguar* makes no effort to conceal the fact that a stuntman was employed as a stand-in for Sabu for the numerous shots showing his character's near-fatal struggle with the snake. For one thing, the snake we see wound around Sabu looks nothing like the snake we see wrapped about the stuntman. Perhaps conveniently, the stuntman's face is completely concealed by the coils of the constrictor, but still there is no mistaking him for Sabu. This scene presents more than a momentary and risible glitch in the film's continuity; it functions as an absolute or irrevocable disruption of *Jaguar*'s somewhat feeble attempts at offering a convincing – if improbable, and perhaps incredible – jungle adventure. Such moments are typical in exploitation films from this period: shots of the has-been and of their stunt-double or stand-in jostle for our attention, as images of each performers' labours are clumsily combined to create the spectacle of the actor's imperilled character. In Ed Wood's *Bride of the Monster/Atom* (1955), for example, there is a sequence which shows the character played by the ageing horror icon Bela Lugosi flailing around some shallows gripped by an 'atomic' but actually rather dilapidated rubber octopus. The shots of Lugosi seizing hold of the rubber tentacles are clearly supplemented by those of a visibly younger and much more energetic stand-in (who is nowhere to be seen in the nostalgic recreation of the shooting of this scene in Tim Burton's *Ed Wood* (1994)).

At this moment in *Jaguar*, the stuntman, in stark contrast to Sabu, appears to be in real danger. Indeed, in his account of the shooting of this scene, Touch Connors (who played Lang) suggests that the snake 'damn near killed [the stuntman]. Three, four guys got in there and grabbed the snake and pried, pried, and got the stuntman loose, and he was almost gone. They barely saved him'.[305] It is of course important to consider the film-makers' exploitation of the stuntman (although I presume he willingly offered them his services), as well as their exploitation of the snake for the purpose of including such a scene in the picture. However, the presentation of Sabu in this sequence is also undoubtedly exploitative. It must privilege the actor's face (at whatever cost to continuity – as had happened in *Elephant Boy*) if it is to capitalise on the star's association with jungle animals – his Mowgli mojo, as it were – and to profit from the star's earlier fame as a genuine 'jungly youth'. However, in 1937, the *New York Times* suggested that *Elephant Boy* was 'one of the most likable of the jungle pictures' precisely because it had 'the wisdom and the good taste' to tell its story 'simply and without recourse to synthetic sensationalism': 'Sabu, its 12-year-old hero, never once is chased by a tiger, embraced by a python or dropped into a swirl of crocodiles.'[306] In *Jaguar*'s shoddy sensationalism, Sabu is required to animate a synthetic python prop in order to create a convincing-enough image of his character's mortal danger. The actor's energy is thus expended specifically so as to provide the illusion of the snake's own power and strength, as well as to present his own character's desperate efforts to overwhelm it. Such moments signify in condensed fashion the star's own situation in this kind of exploitation picture: he is required to labour in such scenes in order to invest the film with his own power, the waning star power of the has-been, the potential profitability of the former star-property. Sabu had of course by this point already worked on several pictures that had required him to interact with rubber snakes. In *The Jungle Book*, for instance, Sabu's Mowgli was ferried through the river by his python friend Kaa, and then grappled with a cobra in the caves beneath the lost city, and in *Cobra Woman,* there is the climactic sequence in which Sabu's character Kado must strangle the Cobra King of Cobra Island. However, in *Jaguar*, there is something much more *desperate* about Juano's struggle with the snake, and not only because the sequence exploits that footage of the stuntman being actually suffocated by the boa constrictor. When Sabu appears to try and chew into the throat of the rubber snake, we watch the actor obliged to *make do*, to make the absolute *most* of whatever was available, whatever was affordable, during the production of the film. The star's performance in this sequence thus embodies the exploitative procedures of the entire picture. Sabu wrings the neck of the rubber snake as convincingly as he can, and, at the same time, the film intends to wring as much value as possible from its star's name, face and effortful labour. *Jaguar* blatantly seeks to exploit Sabu's potential value as a former (and possible future) star of commercially successful pictures, and *can* precisely due to the has-been's increasingly precarious professional status, in which the star's waning appeal impacts on the affordability of their name and the availability of their time.

Eventually, the jaguar-worshipping tribesmen capture Juano and take him to their village. By this point, Juano is utterly convicted that he has already killed several of his party, and has fled from the camp in order to 'return' to the tribe he was removed from as a toddler. After Juano has been captured, the tribesmen prepare his execution, but then they notice a mysterious jaguar-claw-shaped birthmark on his neck. The following shot shows Juano dressed in one of the jaguar-print romper-suits, being given a knife, which he grips in his jaguar-print mitten, and being led towards an altar, where a little black piglet is tethered and waiting. Juano shuffles slowly towards the piglet, raises the knife above his shoulder, a fierce glint in his eye. The tribesmen urge him on, but Juano hesitates. He stares at the piglet, then at his knife, and whispers to himself, 'I can't', before turning to the tribesmen, and shouts 'I CAN'T!', cutting the piglet free; as the tribesmen crowd around him, the piglet trots away, somewhat indignantly.

In this sequence, the film's rampantly racist representation of 'primitive' people and 'tribal' ritual becomes a ridiculous spectacle of ersatz ethnographic trash. These scenes also expose how blatantly the film attempts to exploit its star's popular image. The 'fantastic' story of Juano's discovery and adoption by

Doctor Powell was clearly intended to capitalise on the audience's awareness of the 'incredible' story of the 'discovery' and 'civilising' of Sabu almost twenty years earlier, and the attitudes of characters like Bailey and Lang, moreover, quite closely resemble the racist and colonialist ideas that were perpetuated in the media's initial construction of the star. The film conceals the real identity of the killer in order to create suspense, and thus refuses until the very end to reveal that Juano is not a violent 'savage.' When Bailey and the doctor discuss Juano's background, Bailey expresses the opinion that 'once a savage, always a savage'. Eventually, the film makes it very clear that while Juano was indeed 'once a savage', he isn't one now. However, by so obviously exploiting ideas about Sabu's own background in India, the film exposes how, despite being 'civilised' by being removed from the jungles and becoming a film star, Sabu was to remain associated with the 'savage' (and also the 'subhuman') precisely through being cast repeatedly in roles such as this.

Jungle Hell (1956)

After completing his work on *Jaguar* (and *The Magic Lamp* pilots) in the autumn of 1954, Sabu promptly began working on another television project. In October, *Billboard* reported that the independent producer Norman Cerf had formed a production company, called Taj Mahal Productions, and that over two days in the last week of September the pilot episodes for a television series called *Jungle Boy*, starring Sabu, had been filmed.[307] During the mid-1950s, there were a great many popular television series that centred on jungle danger and adventure, known in the trade as the 'straw hut circuit'.[308] For example, Jon Hall, Sabu's former co-star from the Universal days, starred in *Ramar of the Jungle* (1952–3), and Sabu's hero, Johnny Weissmuller, former star of the *Tarzan* films, starred in *Jungle Jim* (1954–8). (In these shows Indian characters were typically played by white actors, such as Norman Fredic in *Jungle Jim* and Victor Milan in *Ramar of the Jungle*. In the popular television show *Andy's Gang* (1955–60) the Indian characters Ganga and Ram were played by Nino Marcel and Vito Scotti.) However, as had happened with *The Magic Lamp*, the pilot episodes of *Jungle Boy* failed to attract sponsorship, and so no further episodes were made. Sabu was not the only former child star attempting to break into television in the mid-1950s by trading on audiences' memories of his 'jungle boy' persona from a previous era. Johnny Sheffield, who had played the Boy character alongside Weissmuller in the *Tarzan* films during the 1930s, and who had then appeared in the popular *Bomba the Jungle Boy* serials in the 1940s, similarly failed to find sponsorship for his proposed television series *Bantu the Zebra Boy*. Several years later, the two episodes of *Jungle Boy* were combined and made into a feature film, with the title *The Jungle Boy* aka *Jungle Hell*, which was eventually released in theatres in the late 1950s. (Sabu reportedly fought to stop the film being released). The new title was presumably required to differentiate the feature from the 1957 television show *Adventures of a Jungle Boy*, which had aired for one season in 1957, and which centred on the escapades of a young white orphan boy, his cheetah, and a friendly doctor deep in the jungles of Africa. By the early 1960s, a new version of *Jungle Hell* was in circulation, in which scenes showing UFOs hovering over the jungle were added to the original film. A voiceover added to the conclusion of this version of the film explains that the UFOs were responsible for the strange events that had taken place in the jungle, since at no point in the film do any of the characters actually acknowledge let alone refer to the sinister spaceships. Unsurprisingly, perhaps, *Jungle Hell* has become a cult classic, and is celebrated by connoisseurs of exploitation cinema. It is also often listed as among the worst films ever made, and is regularly discussed in online forums devoted to 'bad' cinema.[309] While the 'UFO' version of *Jungle Hell* is the most notorious, due to its awkward incorporation of science-fiction elements, the 'original' version is the one I shall examine here.

Jungle Hell offers further evidence of how, during the 1950s, Sabu's labours were expended on commercial enterprises that failed to function as they were intended. The credit sequence begins with a notice of 'grateful acknowledgment to the Ministry of Information, Division of Films, of the government of India, and to His Highness the Maharajah of Mysore for their aid and co-operation in the production of this motion picture', which, while presumably bogus, is nevertheless incredibly similar to the note of appreciation that appears at the beginning of Sabu's first film, *Elephant Boy*. Then, we are or appear to be in Tangri, deep in the jungles of India, in a television studio, in Hollywood. A small boy (played by Sabu's son, Paul Dastagir) is stretched out upon an altar. Shan-Kar, a Holy Man (Naji) is standing over him, intoning mysteriously. Sabu is standing nearby, watching the child, his hands joined together in prayer, and appears to be dressed in a kind of gigantic nappy. The child's mother, Shusheila (Sarena Sande) sits to one side, gently rocking back and forth and whispering to herself. Sabu kneels down beside her to offer her some exposition: he quietly beseeches her to take the child to one Doctor Morrison (David Bruce), gently explaining that he had recently suffered from the same kinds of burns that now afflict the child and that Doctor Morrison had healed him. She protests that the Holy Man has promised to help her son.

Meanwhile, Kumar (Robert Cabal) tells the Holy Man what Sabu is up to, and warns him that if the child is cured by Doctor Morrison, then the villagers will begin to doubt *his* powers. So the Holy Man forbids it, and ordains that the child must spend the entire night on the altar. That night, a tiger comes prowling onto the village set. The boy is still asleep on the altar, while his mother and Sabu sleep nearby. The tiger slinks about, while stock footage shows a gorilla, apparently watching the tiger. The tiger continues exploring the set, until Sabu is awakened by the gorilla, who begins to honk loudly from her vantage point in the stock footage. Sabu leaps to his feet, pulls out his dagger, and the tiger runs back across the set. Sabu decides no time must be lost, tells Shusheila that the child must be taken to Morrison at once: 'I'll get the elephant!' he says. Sabu runs off to call for Rangar, his elephant. Now it is Kumar, sleeping nearby, who is awakened by the stock footage of an elephant trumpeting loudly, apparently in response to Sabu's cries. Kumar tries to stop them, but Sabu floors him, and leaves with Shusheila and the child. The film then offers more stock footage of someone riding an elephant through the forest, a child is perched on the elephant's back, but there is no sign of Sabu, or Shusheila, or her son. Stock footage shows men working their buffaloes in the fields, apparently nearby. And then even more stock footage follows, a rapid succession of catalogue shots of various animals: a tiger, a panther, some wolves, some monkeys, some deer; back to: the tiger again; now, a warthog; some more deer; and then cut to: a mongoose fighting with a cobra. This *Jungle Book*-style spectacle, wholly derived from stock footage, supplements the studio scenes with the requisite images of wild animals that are required and now repurposed by the jungle show, exploited for their 'genuine' jungle drama. Sabu, too, is being repurposed here: his jungle boy persona is being reactivated, as are our memories of Toomai, and of Mowgli too. In the original television show, and therefore in *Jungle Hell*, Sabu's character is called simply 'Sabu'. The naming of the character after the star reveals how the original show intended to exploit that name, and extract from 'Sabu' (and, of course, Sabu) whatever value it could.

After treating the boy, Doctor Morrison writes a letter to Doctor Caldwell (Ted Stanhope), his former teacher, in London, and describes the 'peculiar subcutaneous inflammation' which, it transpires, is the result of the 'natives' having handled certain rocks exposed by newly uprooted teak trees. Morrison suspects the rocks are contaminated with radioactive uranium, but would appreciate a second opinion. But Doctor Caldwell, upon receipt of the letter, decides to sends his assistant Doctor Pamela Ames (K. T. Stevens) to India in his place. Sabu, meanwhile, is running about the jungle. Some long shots present Sabu running through a real forest, while other, closer shots present Sabu dashing about the studio. Then, a tiger begins to chase after him. Again, some shots present a tiger leaping about the studio, while other shots are stock footage of another tiger, somewhere else. Sabu jumps into a river and begins to swim across, unaware of the wooden crocodile being dragged in his direction. Suddenly, we watch a tiger and a crocodile fighting in a pond somewhere. Sabu makes it to the other side of the river, while in the background the wooden crocodile is being dragged away in the opposite direction. Back in the studio jungle Sabu discovers Doctor Ames; her plane has just crash landed nearby. *Jungle Hell* clearly seeks to replicate the sequence in Sabu's *Jungle Book* in which Shere Khan chases after Mowgli only to be suddenly confronted by a crocodile, but its continual recourse to stock footage, and its blatant disregard for continuity, only emphasise the latter production's relative impoverishment of means and the subsequent diminishment of impact. *Jungle Hell* may appear woefully wanting in many regards when compared with *Jungle Book*, but it nevertheless stars Sabu, the Mowgli of the former film, compensating – by his mere presence, and by his sheer professionalism – for the film's other innumerable shortcomings.

As the narrative continues, we are presented with, or rather bombarded by, an inordinate amount of stock footage, very obviously derived from a diverse range of sources, and which for the remainder of the film presents us with endless scenes of elephants marching slowly through various different forests, filing slowly in and out of various different villages, and hosing themselves down in various different rivers. Compared with the usual and generous deployment of stock footage in the typical exploitation jungle film, such as the piranha footage used periodically in *Jaguar*, the excessive use of such material in *Jungle Hell* is quite literally incredible, often lasting for several minutes at a time. For the most part, the stock footage sequences are inserted between studio sequences, in order to represent the lives of the inhabitants of the village and the surrounding jungles in which the story is taking place. But the stock footage is also more clumsily combined with shots that were filmed in the studio, resulting in ridiculous juxtapositions of dramatic and documentary images. There is Sabu, playing 'Sabu the Jungle Boy', standing somewhere in a jungle set, loudly shouting orders to the natives he is apparently watching driving their elephants down the river. And then there are the elephants, and there is the river, but clearly this has taken place at some earlier time, somewhere else. The film repeats this strategy over and over

Sabu as 'Sabu' in *Jungle Hell* (1956)

again. Kumar tells Sabu that Shan-Kar has gone to the river 'to watch them haul logs for the stockade'; the actor playing Shan-Kar, standing somewhere in the jungle set, watches the elephants hauling the logs for the stockade; and there again are elephants, and they are indeed hauling logs, but very clearly at some earlier time, and in India. The actors here are repeatedly presented standing about, apparently watching elephants, pointing at elephants, and discussing the elephants, explaining to each other what the elephants are doing, but never does a member of the cast ever appear even once in the same shot as an actual elephant.

In the stock footage, we watch *mahouts*, Indian elephant drivers. We see little Indian boys, too, perched on top of their elephants. The makers of the television pilot episodes thus clearly exploited the availability and cheapness of such footage in order to bolster the material that was produced for the show, and relied on this footage to provide the series with much-needed spectacle and a semblance of authenticity. Then, when the episodes were cobbled together for the purpose of producing a feature presentation that could be distributed in theatres, more footage was probably added to extend the running time to an appropriate length. While *Jungle Hell* thus exemplifies the strategies that characterised exploitation cinema, it also evokes for us *Elephant Boy*, produced almost twenty years earlier, which similarly combined the footage shot in India by Flaherty and the sequences produced in the studio in England by Zoltan Korda. Indeed, the stock footage deployed in *Jungle Hell* often focuses on very young 'elephant boys' and such shots resemble quite closely certain scenes featuring Sabu that Flaherty had shot back in 1936. The masses of footage Flaherty brought back to England was used selectively by the film's producers to supplement the new studio scenes in order to produce a film with as much commercial appeal as possible. The Indian footage, therefore, was exploited in order to provide the final film with an illusory basis in reality. *Jungle Hell* thus resembles Sabu's very first film, as the somewhat shoddy artificial studio scenes are punctuated with stock images exploited for their authentic ethnographic spectacle. In *Elephant Boy*, of course, Sabu worked first with Flaherty and then with Korda to produce the scenes that the two directors wanted, and thus appeared in both the 'original' and the 'supplementary' sequences. In *Jungle Hell*'s patently make-do juxtaposition of old stock footage and new studio scenes, however, Sabu of course appears only in the *latter*. As we are reminded by the *former* of the star's childhood in India, it becomes clear that despite the distance between Sabu's early life as a *bona fide* elephant boy in India and his career as an actor in Hollywood, as far as the industry was concerned, he was still, and would remain, for audiences at least, the 'elephant boy' of the movies.

A few years after Sabu's collaboration with Mickey Rooney, in the summer of 1957, Sabu staged another comeback. A newspaper article with the headline 'Sabu, The Elephant Boy, Resumes Acting Career' reported that he had 'two deals in the fire that could bring him back aboard the pachyderms again', and described his 'yen to return to the silver screen and the old "Elephant Boy" roles that no one else can play'.[310] In the early 1960s, Sabu appeared in two major productions, the jungle thriller *Rampage* (1963), with Robert Mitchum, and Disney's family film *A Tiger Walks*, with Pamela Franklin. In both films, Sabu's characters are associated with animals: in *Rampage*, he plays a Malaysian tracker who assists in the hunt led by Mitchum's character and in *A Tiger Walks*, he plays a trainer working with a travelling circus who teams up with a young girl (Franklin) to rescue an escaped tiger.

In the obituaries published following Sabu's sudden death aged 39 in December 1963, he was invariably referred to as 'the elephant boy' or simply 'elephant boy': almost thirty years after the first reports of Flaherty's 'discovery' of Sabu, therefore, the actor was still chiefly associated with the first film on which he worked. In the decades since his death, as I have suggested, certain of the films in which Sabu starred following *Elephant Boy* have become meaningful and pleasurable to different audiences and for different reasons, revered − retrospectively − as either spectacular fantasy, supreme camp or sublime 'trash'. But while the films have now circulated for many years in these heterogeneous contexts, what they have in common is, of course, a performance by Sabu. And while the general contours − and cultural and historical contexts − of Sabu's film career are fairly well known, his performances have rarely received the detailed attention they deserve, despite the contribution that they undoubtedly make to the films on which he worked. As I hope to have demonstrated, Sabu's labours as a star warrant (and reward) our interest precisely due to the way they reveal how he both embraced the opportunities that were made available to him and transcended the fantasies projected onto him, whether during his reign as 'England's greatest boy actor', while working under contract with Universal, or while staging his comeback in the post-studio era.

Notes

Introduction
1. Maurice Yacowar, 'An Aesthetic Defence of the Star System in Films', *Quarterly Review of Film Studies* vol. 4 no. 1, 1979, pp. 41, 46.
2. Edgar Morin, *The Stars*, trans. Richard Howard (Minneapolis and London: University of Minnesota Press, 2005 [1972]), pp. 27–8, 28, emphasis in original.
3. Ibid., p. 89.
4. Yacowar, 'An Aesthetic Defence of the Star System in Films', pp. 46–7.
5. 'Elephants Like His Smile', *Daily Mirror*, 9 December 1935, p. 8.
6. Miklós Rózsa, *Double Life: The Autobiography of Miklós Rózsa* (Tunbridge Wells: Midas Books/New York: Hippocrene Books, 1982), p. 112.
7. Jeremy G. Butler, 'Introduction', in Jeremy G. Butler (ed.), *Star Texts: Image and Performance in Film and Television* (Detroit, MI: Wayne State University Press, 1991), p. 8.
8. Lesley Stern and George Kouvaros, 'Descriptive Acts: Introduction', in Lesley Stern and George Kouvaros (eds), *Falling for You: Essays on Cinema and Performance* (Sydney: Power Publications, 1999), pp. 3, 30.
9. John Ellis, *Visible Fictions: Cinema, Television, Radio*, rev. edn (London and New York: Routledge, 1992 [1982]), p. 99.

Chapter One
10. J. M. Blaut, *The Colonizer's Model of the World: Geographical Diffusionism and Eurocentric History* (New York and London: Guildford Press, 1993), p. 96, emphasis in original.
11. Ibid., p. 96.
12. When Sabu came to England to finish work on *Elephant Boy*, there were very few Indians in the country. The 1932 Indian National Congress survey of 'Indians outside India' suggested that there were just over 7,000 (7,128) Indians living in Britain (which had a total population of about 44 million); the majority lived in the larger

cities, with between 200–300 in London. See Rozina Visram, *Asians in Britain: 400 Years of History* (London and Sterling, VA: Pluto Press, 2002), pp. 254, 262–3. According to Humayan Ansari, it wasn't until the end of World War I that South Asians began to form 'a significant part of the "visible" migrant population'. The interwar period saw a decline in the migration of Indians to Britain (since there was less need for cheap labour) but in the late 1930s the number of economic migrants increased somewhat. See 'Mapping the Colonial: South Asians in Britain, 1857–1947', in N. Ali, S. Kalra and S. Sayyid (eds), *A Postcolonial People: South Asians in Britain* (New York: Columbia University Press, 2008), pp. 143, 152.
13. 'Indian Boy Screen Star', *Times of India*, 2 December 1936, p. 17.
14. 'Sabu's Smile', *Times of India*, 30 December 1936, p. 10.
15. Frank S. Nugent, '*Elephant Boy*', *New York Times*, 6 April 1937.
16. W. W. Robson, 'Introduction', in Rudyard Kipling, *The Jungle Book* (Oxford and New York: Oxford University Press, 1987 [1894]), p. xv.
17. John Lockwood Kipling, *Beast and Man in India* (London and New York: Macmillan, 1891), p. 230.
18. George Peress Sanderson, *Thirteen Years among the Wild Beasts of India: Their Haunts and Habits from Personal Observations; With an Account of the Modes of Capturing and Taming Elephants* (London: W. H. Allen, 1879).
19. Kipling, *Beast and Man in India*, p. 249–50.
20. Rudyard Kipling, *Toomai of the Elephants* (1894) (London: Macmillan, 1937 [1894]), p. 136.
21. Jack Whittingham, *Sabu of the Elephants* (London: Hurst and Blackett, 1938), p. 25.
22. Kracauer (1960) cited in Christopher Williams (ed.), *Realism and the Cinema* (London and Henley: Routledge and Kegan Paul, 1980), p. 101.
23. Frances Hubbard Flaherty, *Elephant Dance* (London: Faber and Faber, 1937), p. 15.
24. Arthur Calder-Marshall, *The Innocent Eye: The Life of Robert Flaherty* (London: W. H. Allen, 1963), p. 177.
25. Richard Barsam, *The Vision of Robert Flaherty: The Artist as Myth and Filmmaker* (Bloomington and Indianapolis: Indiana University Press, 1988), p. 74; see also Calder-Marshall, *The Innocent Eye*, p. 178.
26. Karol Kulik, *Alexander Korda: The Man Who Could Work Miracles* (London: Virgin Books, 1990 [1975]), p. 188.
27. 'When Darkness Falls', *Film Pictorial* vol. 10 no. 241, 3 October 1936, p. 8.
28. Visram, *Asians in Britain*, pp. 259–60.
29. Paul Rotha, *Robert J. Flaherty: A Biography*, ed. Jay Ruby (Philadelphia: University of Pennsylvania Press, 1983), pp. 165, 179.

30. Charles Drazin, *Korda: Britain's Only Movie Mogul* (London: Macmillan, 2002), p. 178.
31. Flaherty, *Elephant Dance*, p. 15.
32. Ibid., p. 14.
33. 'Indian Boy as Kim Hero', *Observer*, 27 January 1935, p. 10.
34. 'Indian Boy as Kim Hero', p. 10.
35. 'Film Expedition in Search of "Elephant Boy"', *Times of India*, 2 February 1935, p. 17.
36. 'Hunt for India's Boy Film Star', *Times of India*, 9 March 1935, p. 19.
37. 'Search for Boy to Take Part of Mahout's Son', *Times of India*, 29 March 1935, p. 12.
38. Ibid.
39. See *Film Pictorial* vol. 13 no. 323, 30 April 1938, pp. 16–17. Most famous, of course, was Selznick's search for an actress to play Scarlett O'Hara in *Gone with the Wind* (1939), which also began in 1936, and which received a great deal of attention in the press. See Helen Taylor, *Scarlett's Women*: Gone with the Wind *and Its Female Fans* (New Brunswick, NJ: Rutgers University Press, 1989), pp. 82–4.
40. 'Palace to Become Cinema Studio', *Times of India*, 2 July 1935, p. 5.
41. Flaherty, *Elephant Dance*, p. 32.
42. Ibid., p. 42.
43. Osmond Borradaile, with Anita Borradaile Hadley, *Life through a Lens: Memoirs of a Cinematographer* (Montreal and Ithaca, NY: McGill-Queen's University Press, 2001), p. 74.
44. Borradaile, *Life through a Lens*, p. 74
45. Ibid.
46. Ibid., pp. 74–5.
47. Flaherty, *Elephant Dance*, p. 46.
48. '*Elephant Boy* Unit's Adventures', *Kinematograph Weekly* no. 1487, 17 October 1935, p. 58.
49. Flaherty, *Elephant Dance*, p. 49.
50. Ibid.
51. 'Mr Flaherty and an Elephant Boy', *New York Times*, 10 November 1935, p. X4.
52. Flaherty, *Elephant Dance*, pp. 49–50.
53. '*Elephant Boy* Unit's Adventures', p. 58.
54. Flaherty, *Elephant Dance*, p. 60.
55. Ibid., p. 74.
56. 'New Film of India', *Times of India*, 11 February 1936, p. 8.
57. 'Keep Them in the Background,' *Film Pictorial* vol. 11 no. 278, 19 June 1936, p. 30–1.
58. Winifred Holmes, 'Celluloid Children', *World Film News* vol. 1 no. 5, August 1936, p. 3.

59. Ibid., p. 3.
60. A Hollywood adaptation of Shakespeare's *A Midsummer Night's Dream*, directed by William Dieterle and Max Reinhardt, was released in 1935; the Indian Prince was, according to the International Movie Database, played by one 'Sheila Brown'. The underground film-maker Kenneth Anger would later claim he had played the role; this legend is perpetuated by, for example, Alice L. Hutchison, *Kenneth Anger: A Demonic Visionary* (London: Black Dog Publishing, 2004), p. 12.
61. Alexander Korda, Foreword, in Whittingham, *Sabu of the Elephants*, p. 10. During this period there were several articles in the press that referred to the British film industry's capacity to compete with Hollywood: for example, in 'Where Are Britain's New Stars?' (*Film Pictorial* vol. 10 no. 248, 21 November 1936, p. 7) concern is expressed about the British studios' failure to discover actors and actresses who could rival their American counterparts at the box office. When it came to the lack of British child stars, however, the magazine argued that the law made it extremely difficult for studios to make films featuring young children. A feature about the rise of the 'teen star' in Hollywood, noting the recent success of Deanna Durbin (aged fourteen) and Mickey Rooney (aged fifteen), commented:

> The rule about employing children under 14 in the studios on this side is still very much in force (a fine is inflicted every time this happens, but even British studios have to portray life sometimes, which means that they have to sneak in a few kids by the back door (William H. Boorne, 'Out Go the Babies, In Come the Youngsters', *Film Pictorial* vol. 11 no. 261, 20 February 1937, p. 17).

Later the same year, in 'British Children Are Not Born until They're Fourteen,' Boorne described in more detail the circumstances under which children worked for the film studios:

> The whole thing has to be kept terribly secret. Only those actually working on the film know that a child is being employed. Advance publicity is banned – until the child has completed her work, at any rate. For if the authorities get to hear that a youngster is being employed, they can – and do – step in and threaten dire penalties if the law is defied. As it is the makers of films are invariably fined for contravening the law' (*Film Pictorial* vol. 12 no. 310, 27 November 1937, p. 10).

The Children and Young Persons Act of 1933 indeed specified that children under the age of fourteen could work no more than two hours on a school day (and no later than seven o'clock in the evening), no more than two hours on a Sunday, and no more than five hours Saturdays; altogether, children should work no more than twelve hours a week (during term time) and no more than twenty-five hours a week (during the holidays).

62. John Grierson, 'The Finest Eyes in Cinema', *World Film News* vol. 1 no. 12, March 1937, p. 5.
63. Ibid.
64. Rotha, *Robert J. Flaherty*, pp. 177–8.
65. 'Impressive Kipling Film at Empire', *Times of India*, 12 June 1937, p. 7.
66. '*Elephant Boy*', *The Times*, 7 April 1937, p. 14.
67. Nelson B. Bell, 'A New Star Looms upon the Screen in Master Sabu, Little East Indian Lad, Who Plays *Elephant Boy*', *Washington Post*, 16 July 1937, p. 12.
68. Guy Morgan, 'Take Your Family to See This Boy', *Daily Express*, 9 April 1937, p. 5. In 1937, Freddie Bartholomew also appeared in a Kipling adaptation, *Captains Courageous*, directed by Victor Fleming and released shortly after *Elephant Boy*. In the summer, Shirley Temple, the most successful child star of the 1930s, starred in another Kipling adaptation, *Wee Willie Winkie*, directed by John Ford.
69. Karen Lury, *The Child in Film: Tears, Fears and Fairy Tales* (London and New York: I. B. Tauris, 2010), p. 151.
70. Ibid., p. 152.
71. Béla Balász, *The Theory of Film*, trans. Edith Bone (London: Dennis Dobson, 1952), pp. 80–1.
72. Ibid., p. 80; Béla Balász, *Béla Balász's Early Film Theory: Visible Man and The Spirit of Film*, trans. Erica Carter and Rodney Livingstone (Oxford: Berghahn Books, 2010), p. 60–1.
73. Balász, *The Theory of Film*, p. 81.
74. Flaherty, *Elephant Dance*, p. 14.
75. '*Elephant Boy*'s Success', *Manchester Guardian*, 15 March 1937, p. 12.
76. Morgan, 'Take Your Family to See This Boy', p. 5.
77. '*Elephant Boy*', *The Times*, 7 April 1937, p. 14.
78. Mae Tinée, '*Elephant Boy* – Good Film of Kipling Story', *Chicago Daily Tribune*, 9 June 1937, p. 17; Henry Gibbs, 'Shows Seen', *Action* no. 61, 17 April 1937, p. 13.
79. Bell, 'A New Star Looms upon the Screen in Master Sabu', p. 12; Nelson B. Bell, 'India Makes Its Contribution to the List of Screen Wonders', *Washington Post*, 18 July 1937, p. 7.
80. Lury, *The Child in Film*, p. 152.
81. Flaherty, *Elephant Dance*, p. 50.

82. 'Impressive Kipling Film at Empire', p. 7; 'Elephant Boy', Kinematograph Weekly no. 1556, 11 February 1937, p. 34.
83. June Provines, 'Front View and Profiles', Chicago Daily Tribune, 22 September 1938, p. 18.
84. Vijay Prashad, The Karma of Brown Folk (Minneapolis and London: University of Minnesota Press, 2000), pp. 27–8.
85. Ibid., p. 29.
86. 'Sabu at the Zoo', Daily Mirror, 6 April 1937, p. 6.
87. See 'News in a Nutshell', British Pathe Gazette, 5 May 1937, available online at: http://www.britishpathe.com/record.php?id=7360 (accessed 16 December 2013).
88. 'The Week at the Zoo', Observer, 25 April 1937, p. 15.
89. John Berger, Why Look at Animals? (London: Penguin, 2009 [1980]), p. 31. See also Randy Malamud, Reading Zoos: Representations of Animals and Captivity (New York: New York University Press, 1998).
90. 'Jungle Friends Didn't Forget', Daily Mirror, 21 June 1937, p. 5.
91. 'Sabu, This Is Billy!', Daily News, New York, 18 September 1938, page unknown.
92. Whittingham, Sabu of the Elephants, p. 119.
93. Ibid.
94. Katherine Roberts, 'Civilizing Sabu of India: The Story of a Jungle Child in a Modern World', Photoplay vol. 53 no. 1, January 1939, p. 24.
95. Theodore Strauss, 'New Arabian Nights: Sabu, the Elephant Boy, Today Travels via a Twin-Motored Flying Carpet', New York Times, 15 September 1940, p. 35.
96. 'Tea from the Empire', The Times, 11 January 1939, p. 7. An association between Sabu and tea is also suggested by the range of 'Sabu Ware' produced by Colclough China Ltd shortly after the release of Elephant Boy, including a teapot in the shape of an elephant – with Sabu kneeling on the elephant's shoulders and functioning as the handle of the lid – and cups, saucers and plates decorated with cartoons showing Sabu riding elephants and flying carpets. Sabu visited the factory in Stoke-on-Trent, Staffordshire, to promote the launch of the range.
97. The rise of Indian nationalism was a major source of political and intellectual debate during the 1930s. The 1935 Government of India Act, which conceded some autonomy to the provinces, ultimately functioned, according to Ronald Hyam, as a 'mechanism for ensuring the survival of the Raj by creating a buffer of collaborators'. Hyam writes:

> Within five years, British Policy in India was in disarray, the whole situation was deadlocked, and imperial prestige in India at its nadir. Thus British Indian policy in the

1930s is unequivocal evidence of a dysfunctional empire. The transfer of power in 1947 was, on any objective criterion, at least ten years too late. (*Britain's Declining Empire: The Road to Decolonisation, 1918–1968*, Cambridge: Cambridge University Press, 2006, p. 65).

98. 'Sabu', *Western Mail*, 29 September 1936, p. 3.
99. Bill Ashcroft, *On Post-Colonial Futures: Transformations of Colonial Culture* (London and New York: Continuum, 2001), p. 36.
100. Ibid., pp. 36–7, 39.
101. Ashis Nandy, 'The Psychology of Colonialism: Sex, Age and Ideology in British India', in Stephen Howe (ed), *The New Imperial Histories Reader* (London and New York: Routledge, 2010), p. 129.
102. Ibid, p. 131.
103. Frances Flaherty and Ursula Leacock, *Sabu the Elephant Boy* (London: J. M. Dent and Sons, Ltd, 1937).
104. Ariel Dorfman, *The Empire's Old Clothes: What the Lone Ranger, Babar, and Other Innocent Heroes Do to Our Minds* (New York: Pantheon Books, 1983), p. 40.
105. Ibid., pp. 19, 25.
106. Stephen O'Harrow, 'Babar and the *Mission Civilisatrice*: Colonialism and the Biography of a Mythical Elephant', *Biography* vol. 22 no. 1, Winter 1999, pp. 95–6.
107. Jean De Brunhoff, *The Story of Babar the Little Elephant*, trans. Merle S. Haas (New York: Random House, 1933 [1931]), p. 3.
108. Flaherty and Leacock, *Sabu the Elephant Boy*, p. 10; see also Whittingham, *Sabu of the Elephants*, p. 10.
109. De Brunhoff, *The Story of Babar the Little Elephant*, pp. 14–15.
110. Ibid., p. 22.
111. Ibid., p. 18.
112. Ashcroft, *On Post-Colonial Futures*, p. 43.
113. 'Sabu's Smile', p. 10.
114. Whittingham, *Sabu of the Elephants*, p. 118.
115. Anne McClintock, *Imperial Leather: Race, Gender and Sexuality in the Colonial Contest* (New York and London: Routledge, 1995), p. 214.
116. Ibid., p. 223.
117. *Filmindia* vol. 3 no. 11, March 1938, p. 21.
118. '*Elephant Boy's* Success', p. 12.
119. Whittingham, *Sabu of the Elephants*, p. 90.
120. Morgan, 'Take Your Family to See This Boy', p. 8.

121. Roberts, 'Civilizing Sabu of India', p. 24.
122. David Flaherty, 'Sabu', *World Film News* vol. 2 no. 1, April 1937, p. 11.
123. Exhibitor's Campaign Book for *The Drum*, 1938, no page.
124. *Cinegram* no. 25, 1938, no page.
125. Ibid.
126. 'Sabu as an Indian Prince in a Colourful Story of the North-West Frontier', *Film Pictorial* vol. 13 no. 320, 9 April 1938, p. 25.
127. Jeffrey Richards, *Visions of Yesterday* (London: Routledge, 1973), p. 220.
128. Whittingham, *Sabu of the Elephants*, p. 89.
129. Ibid.
130. Ibid., p. 113.
131. *Cinegram* no. 25, 1938, no page.
132. 'When East Meets West End', *Australian Women's Weekly*, 22 May 1937, p. 51.
133. O'Harrow, 'Babar and the *Mission Civilisatrice*', p. 100.
134. Shompa Lahiri, *Indians in Britain: Anglo-Indian Encounters, Race and Identity, 1880–1930* (London and Portland, OR: Frank Cass, 2000), p. 82.
135. Ibid., pp. 110, 92–3.
136. Ibid., p. 94.
137. Ibid., p. 110.
138. Frank Richards, 'Aliens at Greyfriars', *Magnet* vol. 1 no. 6, 21 March 1908.
139. Despite his 'dusky complexion' the Nabob of Bhanipur is not to be confused with other 'aliens': the readers of the *Magnet* are addressed on this issue:

    My dear boys, there is as much difference between a Hindu or the warrior races and a nigger as between say, you and an Eskimo! The higher races of India are of the same Aryan stock as ourselves ('Greyfriars Gallery', *Magnet* vol. 11 no. 483, 12 May 1917).

140. Whittingham, *Sabu of the Elephants*, pp. 111–13.
141. Ibid., p. 113.
142. See, for example, Whittingham, *Sabu of the Elephants*, p. 113. Sabu sometimes said he would like to become a professional ice-skater if his career in films was to come to an end. There are during this period several references in the press to the Indian boy's admiration for Sonja Henie, the Norwegian ice-skater (winner of the gold medal at the Olympics in 1926, 1932 and 1936), who began making winter-sports-themed-musicals for 20th Century-Fox at this time. Among Henie's films are *One in a Million*, directed by Sidney Lanfield, 1936, *Thin Ice*, also directed by Lanfield, 1937, and *Happy Landing*, directed by Roy Del Ruth, 1938. Sabu even intimated that his

ambition was to make a film with her. See John K. Newnham's profile of Sabu, 'Sidelight on Sabu', in *Film Weekly* vol. 20 no. 524, 29 October 1938, p. 23, and Provines, 'Front View and Profiles', p. 18.
143. Exhibitors' Campaign Book for *The Drum*, 1938, no page.
144. Whittingham, *Sabu of the Elephants*, p. 113.
145. C. A. Lejeune, *Observer*, 19 July 1936, p. 12.
146. *Boy's Life* vol. 27 no. 5, May 1937, p. 20.
147. 'Sabu: Elephant Boy of the Films', *The Times*, 4 December 1963, p. 18.
148. Ibid., my emphasis.
149. 'Sabu the Elephant Boy Is Dead', *New York Times*, 3 December 1963, p. 43.
150. Bell, 'India Makes Its Contribution to the List of Screen Wonders', p. 7.

Chapter Two
151. Charles Drazin, 'Korda, Technicolor and the Zeitgeist', *Journal of British Cinema and Television* vol. 7 no. 1, April 2010, p. 5.
152. Sarah Street, *Colour Films in Britain: The Negotiation of Innovation, 1900–55* (London: BFI, 2012), p. 55.
153. Fred E. Basten, *Glorious Technicolor: The Movies' Magic Rainbow* (South Brunswick, NJ and New York: A. S. Barnes and Co., 1980), p. 63.
154. Ibid., p. 102.
155. Ibid.
156. Sarah Berry, 'Hollywood Exoticism', in Lucy Fischer and Marcia Landy (eds), *Stars: The FILM Reader* (New York and London: Routledge, 2004), pp. 192–3.
157. 'She's Colourful', *Film Pictorial* vol. 10 no. 238, 12 September 1938, p. 14.
158. Steve Neale, *Cinema and Technology: Image, Sound, Colour* (London: BFI, 1985), p. 155.
159. Strauss, 'New Arabian Nights', p. 35, my emphasis.
160. Scott Higgins, *Harnessing the Technicolor Rainbow: Colour Design in the 1930s* (Austin: University of Texas Press, 2007), p. 88.
161. Ibid., p. 87.
162. Richard W. Haines, *Technicolor Movies: The History of Dye Transfer Printing* (Jefferson: McFarland and Co., 1993), p. 35.
163. Richard Misek, *Chromatic Cinema: A History of Screen Colour* (Chichester: Wiley-Blackwell, 2010), p. 38.
164. Homi K. Bhabha, *The Location of Culture* (London and New York: Routledge, 1994), p. 78.
165. Ibid., p. 79.

166. Misek, *Chromatic Cinema*, p. 31.
167. Shirley R. Simpson, 'A Plea for Natural Colour', *Kinematograph Weekly*, 26 August 1937, p. 4, cited in Street, *Colour Films in Britain*, p. 51.
168. Basten, *Glorious Technicolor*, p. 125.
169. 'New Films in London', *The Times*, 6 September 1943, p. 8.
170. John M. MacKenzie, *Propaganda and Empire: The Manipulation of British Public Opinion* (Manchester and New York: Manchester University Press, 1984), pp. 91, 68–9.
171. Jeffrey Richards, '"Patriotism with Profit": British Imperial Cinema in the 1930s', in James Curran and Vincent Porter (eds), *British Cinema History* (London: Weidenfeld and Nicolson, 1983), pp. 245–6, 251.
172. Sarah Street, *British National Cinema* (London and New York: Routledge, 1997), p. 43.
173. Dallas Bower, 'British Films in the Orient', *Great Britain and the East*, 24 June 1937, p. 909, cited in Priya Jaikumar, *Cinema at the End of Empire: A Politics of Transition in Britain and India* (Durham, NC and London: Duke University Press, 2006), p. 141.
174. Cited in Luke McKernan, '"The Modern Elixir of Life": Kinemacolor, Royalty and the Delhi Durbar', *Film History* vol. 21 no. 2, 2009, p. 132.
175. Edward Said, *Orientalism: Western Conceptions of the Orient* (London: Penguin, 1995 [1978]), pp. 5, 6.
176. Ibid., p. 6.
177. Jeffrey Richards, 'Boy's Own Empire: Feature Films and Imperialism in the 1930s', in John M. MacKenzie (ed.), *Imperialism and Popular Culture* (Manchester and New York: Manchester University Press, 1986), p. 143.
178. *The Story of United Artists Product 1937–1938: The Book of the Year*, 1939, no page.
179. Guy Morgan, '*The Drum*', *Daily Express*, 6 April 1938, p. 10; *Saturday Review* no. 4306, 16 April 1938, p. 242.
180. R. Ewart Williams, 'Korda Begins a New Career', *Film Pictorial*, 10 December 1938, p. 13.
181. Whittingham, *Sabu of the Elephants*, p. 99.
182. Powell travelled to Burma to conduct research for *Burmese Silver*, but the film was never completed due to the outbreak of the war.
183. 'Mr. Korda's Plans – A New Eastern Cycle', *Manchester Guardian*, 16 June 1938, p. 12.
184. Morgan, '*The Drum*', p. 10.
185. '*The Drum*', *Manchester Guardian*, 6 April 1938, p. 96.

186. 'Sabu as an Indian Prince in a Colourful Story of the North-West Frontier', pp. 14–15, 25.
187. Ella Shohat and Robert Stam, 'The Imperial Imaginary', in Graeme Turner (ed.), *The Film Cultures Reader* (London and New York: Routledge, 2002), p. 373.
188. Street, *British National Cinema*, p. 44.
189. Prem Chowdhry, *Colonial India and the Making of Empire Cinema: Image, Ideology and Identity* (Manchester and New York: Manchester University Press, 2000), pp. 57, 64.
190. *Times of India*, 7 September 1935, p. 9.
191. David Flaherty, 'Sabu', *World Film News* vol. 2 no. 1, April 1937, p. 11.
192. 'The Life Story of Sabu', *Picture Show* vol. 48 no. 1229, 29 January 1944, p. 11.
193. Louella Parsons, 'Sabu – the 1940 Thief of Bagdad – an Accomplished Actor', *Washington Post*, 20 October 1940, p. A1.
194. *Filmindia* vol. 5 no. 9, September 1939, p. 33.
195. Ibid.
196. The *Filmindia* campaign against 'anti-Indian' films also focused on Richard Eichberg's *The Tiger of Eschnapur* (*Der Tiger von Eschnapur*, 1938), see *Filmindia* vol. 4 no. 5, September 1938, pp. 3–5, and George Stevens's *Gunga Din* (1939), see *Filmindia* vol. 5 no. 2, February 1939, pp. 26–7, 31.
197. Baburao Patel, Editorial, *Filmindia* vol. 4 no. 5, September 1938, p. 3.
198. Victor Small, 'Démarche of Time', *Left Review* vol. 3 no. 16, May 1938, p. 1003.
199. Chowdhry, *Colonial India and the Making of Empire Cinema*, p. 89.
200. Jaikumar, *Cinema at the End of Empire*, pp. 149, 157.
201. Ibid., p. 159. See also Julie Codell, 'Blackface, Faciality, and Colonial Nostalgia in 1930s Empire Cinema', in Sandra Ponzanesi and Marguerite Waller (eds), *Postcolonial Cinema Studies* (London and New York: Routledge, 2012), p. 37.
202. Street, *Colour Films in Britain*, pp. 138, 139.
203. Richard Dyer, 'Resistance through Charisma: Rita Hayworth and *Gilda*', in E. Ann Kaplan (ed.), *Women in Film Noir* (London: BFI, 1980), p. 92.
204. Ibid.
205. 'The Films Provide a Christmas Pantomime', *Picture Post* vol. 9 no. 11, 14 December 1940, p. 31; James Howard, *Michael Powell* (London: B. T. Batsford, 1996), p. 34.
206. Drazin, 'Korda, Technicolor and the Zeitgeist', p. 18. Similarly, Marcia Landy suggests the film 'celebrates aristocracy, responsible authority, exceptional human beings, and the defeat of illegitimate seekers of power' (*British Genres: Cinema and Society, 1930–1960*, Princeton, NJ: Princeton University Press, 1991, p. 110).

207. Bosley Crowther, '*Arabian Nights*', *New York Times*, 26 December 1942, available online at: http://www.nytimes.com/movie/review?res=9C0CE1DC143FE33BBC 4E51DFB4678389659EDE (accessed 16 December 2013).
208. C. A. Lejeune, 'The Films', *Observer,* 22 December 1940, p. 3.
209. Robert Irwin, '*A Thousand and One Nights* at the Movies', *Middle Eastern Literature* vol. 7 no. 2, July 2004, p. 231.
210. Michael Powell, *A Life in Movies: An Autobiography* (London: Heinemann, 1986), p. 581.
211. '*The Thief of Bagdad*', *Picture Show*, 8 March 1941, p. 17.
212. Andrew Moor, '*The Thief of Bagdad*: Arabian Fantasies', 26 May 2008, available online at: www.criterion.com/current/posts/496-the-thief-of-bagdad-arabian-fantasies (accessed 16 December 2013).
213. Landy, *British Genres*, p. 110.
214. C. A. Lejeune, 'New Films in London', *The Times*, 23 December 1940, p. 6.
215. Bosley Crowther, '*The Thief of Bagdad*', *New York Times*, 6 December 1940, available online at: http://www.nytimes.com/movie/review?res= EE05E7DF173AE 477BC4E53DFB467838B659EDE (accessed 16 December 2013).
216. Moor, '*The Thief of Bagdad*'.
217. Peter Hollindale, *Signs of Childness in Children's Books* (Stroud: Thimble Press, 1997), p. 45.
218. Ibid., p. 46.
219. Ibid., p. 47.
220. Ibid.
221. 'A Kipling Jungle Is Re-created', *New York Times Magazine*, 8 March 1942, p. 14.
222. Ibid.
223. Winsten Archer, '*Rudyard Kipling's Jungle Book* Opens at the Rivoli Theatre', *New York Post*, 6 April 1942, p. 62.
224. 'Korda's Brilliant Film of Kipling's *The Jungle Book*', *Today's Cinema* vol. 58 no. 4732, 5 June 1942, pp. 1, 27.
225. Edwin Schallert, 'Sabu to Be "Tough" in New Jungle Role', *Los Angeles Times*, 26 September 1938, p. 16.
226. Strauss, 'New Arabian Nights', p. 35.
227. Bosley Crowther, '*Jungle Book*', *New York Times*, 6 April 1942, available online at: http://www.nytimes.com/movie/review?res=9E04EEDF173AE33BBC4E53 DFB2668389659EDE (accessed 16 December 2013).

Chapter Three

228. '*Cobra Woman*', *Today's Cinema* vol. 62 no. 5037, 26 May 1943, p. 20.
229. Otis L. Guernsey Jr, '*Cobra Woman*', *New York Herald Tribune*, 18 May 1944, reprinted in *New York Motion Picture Critics' Review 1944* vol. 1 no. 33, p. 370.
230. Winsten Archer, 'Animal Kingdom Congregates in *Cobra Woman* at Criterion', *New York Post*, 18 May 1944, reprinted in *New York Motion Picture Critics' Review 1944* vol. 1 no. 33, p. 370.
231. C. A. Lejeune, 'New Films in London', *The Times*, 6 September 1943, p. 8.
232. John T. McManus, 'Sarongs Don't Make a Right', *New York Newspaper PM*, 18 May 1944, reprinted in *New York Motion Picture Critics' Review 1944* vol. 1 no. 33, p. 371.
233. Jim O'Connor, 'Jungle Film at Criterion', *New York Journal-American*, 18 May 1944, reprinted in *New York Motion Picture Critics' Review 1944* vol. 1 no. 33, p. 371.
234. 'The Life Story of Sabu', p. 11.
235. Andrew Ross, *No Respect: Intellectuals and Popular Culture* (New York and London: Routledge, 1989), p. 136.
236. Ibid., p. 146.
237. Ibid., p. 151.
238. Ibid., p. 139.
239. Ibid., p. 151, emphasis in original.
240. Genevieve Waller, '*Cobra Woman*', *Quarterly Review of Film and Video* vol. 27 no. 5, October 2010, pp. 379, 381.
241. Ibid., pp. 381, 380.
242. Michael Moon, 'Flaming Closets', *October* no. 51, Winter 1989, p. 44.
243. Jerry Tartaglia, 'The Perfect Queer Appositeness of Jack Smith', *Quarterly Review of Film and Video* vol. 18 no. 1, 2001, p. 39.
244. Jaikumar, *Cinema at the End of Empire*, p. 150.
245. Bidgood has said:

> I was too young to remember exactly when I was first seduced by [*The*] *Thief of Bagdad*. For years I wasn't certain whether it was something I had dreamed or had actually seen … . It's impossible to describe the impact such opulent imagery had on the relatively colorless existence of this scrawny ragtag first grader … . For 12 cents I was transported to a place where dawns must have been made, where rouged and red lipped lovelies with half veiled faces like a mist of chiffon lounged around turquoise pools, their Technicolor flesh almost covered by bits of satin vests and gossamer harem pants, all surrounded by palace walls made from what seemed to be pink

frosting ice (James Bidgood, Introduction to *The Thief of Bagdad* at the IFC Film Centre in New York, 11 October 2010).

See also Fredric Edgecomb, 'Camping Out with James Bidgood: The Auteur of *Pink Narcissus* Tells All', *Bright Lights Film Journal* no. 52, May 2006, available online at: http://www.brightlightsfilm.com/52/bidgoodiv.php (accessed 16 December 2013).

246. Ryan Powell has discussed the influence of *The Thief of Bagdad* and Universal's costume fantasies on Bidgood's film in 'Dressing *Pink Narcissus*', in Marketa Uhlirova (ed.), *Birds of Paradise: Costume as Cinematic Spectacle* (London: Walther Koenig, 2013), pp. 305–16.
247. Jeffery P. Dennis, *We Boys Together: Teenagers in Love before Girl-Craziness* (Nashville, TN: Vanderbilt University Press, 2007), p. 201.
248. Ibid., p. 203.
249. Ibid., p. 202.
250. See Dominic Johnson, 'The Deaths of Maria Montez', in *Glorious Catastrophe: Jack Smith, Performance and Visual Culture* (Manchester and New York: Manchester University Press, 2012), pp. 142–66.
251. Jack Smith, 'The Perfect Filmic Appositeness of Maria Montez', in J. Hoberman and Edward Leffingwell (eds), *Wait for Me at the Bottom of the Pool: The Writings of Jack Smith* (New York and London: Serpent's Tail, 1997), p. 32.
252. Ibid., p. 32, p. 26.
253. Ibid., p. 25.
254. Ibid.
255. Richard Dyer, *Heavenly Bodies: Film Stars and Society* (Basingstoke and London: Macmillan, 1986), p. 181.
256. Ibid., p. 183.
257. Wade Jennings, 'Nova: Garland in *A Star is Born*', *Quarterly Review of Film Studies* vol. 4 no. 3, Summer 1979, p. 324, cited in Dyer, *Heavenly Bodies*, p. 181.
258. Richard Maltby, *Hollywood Cinema: An Introduction* (Oxford and Malden: Blackwell, 1995), p. 88.
259. Paul Robbins, 'Pax Disney: The Annotated Diary of a Film Extra in India', in Tim Cresswell and Deborah Dixon (eds), *Engaging Film: Geographies of Mobility and Identity* (Lanham, MD: Rowman and Littlefield, 2002), p. 169.
260. Dyer, *Heavenly Bodies*, p. 178.
261. Brett Farmer, *Spectacular Passions: Cinema, Fantasy, Gay Male Spectatorships* (Durham, NC and London: Duke University Press, 2000), pp. 113, 126, 133.

262. Jack Babuscio, 'Camp and the Gay Sensibility', in David Bergman (ed.), *Camp Grounds: Style and Homosexuality* (Amherst: University of Massachusetts Press, 1993), p. 20.
263. Dennis, *We Boys Together*, p. 203.
264. Ibid.
265. Lutz Koepnick reads *Cobra Woman* in relation to the director Robert Siodmak's exile from Germany, and argues that the 'exotic settings clearly mirror Nazi constellations, while the figure of the double sheds light on competing formations of modern society, on what distinguishes liberal from antiliberal solutions to severe political crises' (Lutz Koepnick, 'Doubling the Double: Robert Siodmak in Hollywood', *New German Critique* no. 89, Spring–Summer 2003, pp. 81–104, p. 97).
266. Dyer, *Heavenly Bodies*, p. 183.
267. José Muñoz, *Disidentifications: Queers of Colour and the Performance of Politics* (Minneapolis and London: University of Minnesota Press, 1999), pp. 10, 12, my emphasis.

Chapter Four

268. 'Earl Carroll Spot Reopens', *Billboard*, 13 January 1951, p. 42.
269. For example, Newnham, 'Sidelight on Sabu', p. 23.
270. See Provines, 'Front View and Profiles', p. 18.
271. 'Harringay Arena: Tom Arnold's Circus', *The Times*, 21 December 1951, p. 2.
272. Richard deCordova, *Picture Personalities: The Emergence of the Star System in America* (Urbana: University of Illinois Press, 1990), p. 141.
273. 'English Dancer Accuses Sabu as Father of Child', *Los Angeles Times*, 24 May 1949, p. 2.
274. 'Lived in Sabu's Room, Dancer Says in Court', *Chicago Daily Tribune*, 11 October 1950, p. 9.
275. 'Dancer at Sabu Trial Denies Affair in Egypt', *Los Angeles Times*, 14 October 1950, p. 10.
276. Ibid.
277. Seymour Korman, 'Tigers, Women, and Love Won't Mix, Sabu Says', *Chicago Daily Tribune*, 17 October 1950, p. 4.
278. Ibid.
279. Ibid.
280. 'Sabu, on Stand, Denies Being Father of Child', *Los Angeles Times*, 17 October 1950, p. 8.

281. 'Verdict of Jury Clears Sabu in Paternity Suit', *Los Angeles Times*, 19 October 1950, pp. 1, 12
282. Ibid.
283. Adrienne L. McLean, 'Introduction', in Adrienne L. McLean and David A. Cook (eds), *Headline Hollywood: A Century of Film Scandal* (New Brunswick, NJ and London: Rutgers University Press, 2001), p. 2.
284. Korman, 'Tigers, Women, and Love Won't Mix', p. 4.
285. In March 1952, the paternity case was reopened: the *Los Angeles Times* reported that in a unanimous decision the District Court of Appeal reversed the earlier Superior Court ruling and that the appellate court had ordered a new trial ('Decision Reopens Case against Sabu', *Los Angeles Times*, 21 March 1952, p. 17). The report stated that Julier's attorneys charged that during the original trial Sabu's attorney 'had used the tactic of putting the dancer on trial instead of defending Sabu against her charges', and 'had falsely insinuated the dancer was a loose woman and that his questioning of her was designed to prejudice the jury in that belief'. In July 1953, newspapers reported that Sabu had reached an out-of-court settlement with Mrs Ernst, and had agreed to contribute toward the support of the child, and also pay her legal expenses related to the original trial, but without admitting paternity. This decision was reached on the very day that the second hearing was scheduled to begin. The *Los Angeles Times* reported that the agreement stated that none of its terms should be construed as an admission of paternity ('Sabu Denies Paternity but Agrees to Aid Child', *Los Angeles Times*, 16 July 1953, p. 15).
286. '"Elephant Boy" Returns', *Times of India*, 20 October 1953, p. 3.
287. Gayatri Chatterjee, *Mother India* (London: BFI, 2002), pp. 19–20.
288. 'The Social Whirl: Elephant Boy Comes to Town', *Times of India*, 25 October 1953, p. 11.
289. 'Bombay Calling', *Filmindia* vol. 20 no. 2, February 1954, p. 22.
290. *Filmindia* vol. 20 no. 3, March 1954, p. 87.
291. Ibid., p. 48.
292. Ibid., p. 13.
293. Ibid., p. 40.
294. Ibid., p. 46.
295. Ibid., p. 77.
296. *Filmindia* vol. 20 no. 5, May 1954, p. 21.
297. Ibid.
298. *Filmindia* vol. 20 no. 6, June 1954, p. 16.

299. Jeffrey Sconce, '"Trashing" the Academy: Taste, Excess, and an Emerging Politics of Cinematic Style', *Screen* vol. 36 no. 4, Winter 1995, pp. 376, 374, 372.
300. Paul Watson, 'There's No Accounting for Taste: Exploitation Cinema and the Limits of Film Theory', in Deborah Cartmell, I. Q. Hunter, Heidi Kaye and Imelda Whelehan (eds), *Trash Aesthetics: Popular Culture and Its Audience* (London and Chicago, IL: Pluto Press, 1997), p. 76.
301. '*Jaguar*', *Variety*, 23 April 1956, no page.
302. Gary Hentzi, 'Little Cinema of Horrors', *Film Quarterly* vol. 46 no. 3, Spring 1993, pp. 25, 26.
303. 'Rooney Firm Plans Three Film Series', *Billboard*, 10 July 1954, p. 7.
304. 'Rooney Preps *Tokyo*, *Magic Lamp* Kickoffs', *Billboard*, 24 July 1954, pp. 7, 31.
305. Tom Weaver, *Eye on Science Fiction: 20 Interviews with Classic SF and Horror Filmmakers* (Jefferson, NC, and London: McFarland & Company, Inc., 2007), pp. 23–4.
306. Frank S. Nugent, '*Elephant Boy*', *New York Times*, 6 April 1937, available online at: http://www.nytimes.com/movie/review?res=9906E7D6123AE23ABC4E53DFB266838C629EDE (accessed 16 December 2013).
307. 'Surf Sets up Taj Mahal Co.', *Billboard*, 2 October 1954, p. 2.
308. Winston Wheeler Dixon, *Lost in the Fifties: Recovering Phantom Hollywood* (Carbondale: Southern Illinois University Press, 2005), p. 37.
309. See, for example, Kenn Begg, 'Jungle Hell', *Jabootu's Bad Movie Dimension*, 14 September 2000, available online at: http://www.jabootu.com/junglehell.htm (accessed 16 December 2013); Andrew Borntreger, 'Jungle Hell,' no date, *BADMOVIES.ORG*, available online at: http://www.badmovies.org/movies/junglehell/ (accessed 16 December 2013).
310. Bob Thomas, 'Sabu, The Elephant Boy, Resumes Acting Career', *Hartford Courant*, 11 August 1957, p. 6.

Bibliography

Ansari, Humayan, 'Mapping the Colonial: South Asians in Britain, 1857–1947', in N. Ali, S. Kalra and S. Sayyid (eds), *A Postcolonial People: South Asians in Britain* (New York: Columbia University Press, 2008), pp. 143–56.

Archer, Winsten, 'Rudyard Kipling's "Jungle Book" Opens at the Rivoli Theatre', *New York Post*, 6 April 1942, p. 62.

Archer, Winsten, 'Animal Kingdom Congregates in *Cobra Woman* at Criterion', *New York Post*, 18 May 1944, reprinted in *New York Motion Picture Critics' Review 1944* vol. 1 no. 33, p. 370.

Ashcroft, Bill, *On Post-Colonial Futures: Transformations of Colonial Culture* (London and New York: Continuum, 2001).

Babuscio, Jack, 'Camp and the Gay Sensibility', in David Bergman (ed.), *Camp Grounds: Style and Homosexuality* (Amherst: University of Massachusetts Press, 1993), pp. 19–38.

Balász, Béla, *The Theory of Film*, trans. Edith Bone (London: Dennis Dobson, 1952).

Balász, Béla, *Béla Balász's Early Film Theory: Visible Man and The Spirit of Film*, trans. Erica Carter and Rodney Livingstone (Oxford: Berghahn Books, 2010).

Barnes, Leonard, *Empire or Democracy? A Study of the Colonial Question* (London: Victor Gollancz Ltd, 1939).

Barsam, Richard, *The Vision of Robert Flaherty: The Artist as Myth and Filmmaker* (Bloomington and Indianapolis: Indiana University Press, 1988).

Basten, Fred E., *Glorious Technicolor: The Movies' Magic Rainbow* (South Brunswick, NJ and New York: A. S. Barnes and Co., 1980).

Begg, Kenn, 'Jungle Hell', *Jabootu's Bad Movie Dimensions*, 14 September 2000, available online at: http://www.jabootu.com/junglehell.htm.

Bell, Nelson B., 'A New Star Looms upon the Screen in Master Sabu, Little East Indian Lad, Who Plays "'Elephant Boy'"', *Washington Post*, 16 July 1937, p. 12.

Bell, Nelson B., 'India Makes Its Contribution to the List of Screen Wonders', *Washington Post*, 18 July 1937, p. 7.

Bell, Nelson B., '"Elephant Boy" Registers Hit at the Rialto', *Washington Post*, 19 July 1937, p. 14.

Berger, John, *Why Look at Animals?* (London: Penguin, 2009 [1980]).

Berry, Sarah, 'Hollywood Exoticism', in Lucy Fischer and Marcia Landy (eds), *Stars: The FILM Reader* (New York and London: Routledge, 2004), pp. 181–98.

Bhabha, Homi K., *The Location of Culture* (London and New York: Routledge, 1994).

Bidgood, James, Introduction to *The Thief of Bagdad*, IFC Film Centre, New York, 11 October 2010.

Blaut, J. M., *The Colonizer's Model of the World: Geographical Diffusionism and Eurocentric History* (New York and London: Guildford Press, 1993).

Boorne, William H., 'Out Go the Babies, In Come the Youngsters', *Film Pictorial* vol. 11 no. 261, 20 February 1937, p. 17.

Boorne, William H., 'British Children Are Not Born until They're Fourteen', *Film Pictorial* vol. 12 no. 310, 27 November 1937, p. 10.

Bordwell, David, 'Technicolor', in David Bordwell, Janet Staiger and Kristen Thompson, *The Classical Hollywood Cinema: Film Style and Mode of Production to 1960* (London: Routledge, 1988), pp. 353–7.

Borntreger, Andrew, '*Jungle Hell*', no date, BADMOVIES.ORG, available online at: http://www.badmovies.org/movies/junglehell/ (accessed 16 December 2013).

Borradaile, Osmond, with Anita Borradaile Hadley, *Life through a Lens: Memoirs of a Cinematographer* (Montreal and Ithaca, NY: McGill-Queen's University Press, 2001).

Butler, Jeremy G., 'Introduction', in Jeremy G. Butler (ed.), *Star Texts: Image and Performance in Film and Television* (Detroit, MI: Wayne State University Press, 1991), pp. 7–17.

Calder-Marshall, Arthur, *The Innocent Eye: The Life of Robert Flaherty* (London: W. H. Allen, 1963).

Cannadine, David, *Ornamentalism: How the British Saw Their Empire* (London: Penguin, 2001).

Carroll, Noël, 'Keaton: Film Acting as Action', in Carole Zucker (ed.), *Making Visible the Invisible: An Anthology of Original Essays on Film Acting* (London: Scarecrow Press, 1990), pp. 198–223.

Chandrasekhar, S., 'Indian Immigration in America', *Far Eastern Survey* vol. 13 no. 15, 26 July 1944, pp. 138–43.

Chandrasekhar, S., 'The Indian Community in the United States,' *Far Eastern Survey* vol. 14 no. 11, 6 June 1945, pp. 147–9.

Chapman, John, 'Sabu's Story a Veritable Magic Carpet Tale', *Chicago Daily Tribune*, 11 August 1940, p. 3.

Chatterjee, Gayatri, *Mother India* (London: BFI, 2002).

Chowdhry, Prem, *Colonial India and the Making of Empire Cinema: Image, Ideology and Identity* (Manchester and New York: Manchester University Press, 2000).

Codell, Julie, 'Blackface, Faciality, and Colonial Nostalgia in 1930s Empire Cinema', in Sandra Ponzanesi and Marguerite Waller (eds), *Postcolonial Cinema Studies* (London and New York: Routledge, 2012), pp. 32–46.

Cook, Alton, 'There's a Variety of Corn in New Criterion Picture', *New York World-Telegram*, 17 May 1944, reprinted in *New York Motion Picture Critics' Review 1944* vol. 1 no. 33, p. 370.

Crowther, Bosley, 'The Elephant Boy in Modern Dress', *New York Times*, 18 September 1938, p. 159.

Crowther, Bosley, '*Jungle Book*', *New York Times*, 6 April 1942, available online at: http://movies.nytimes.com/movie/review?res=9E04EEDF173AE33BBC4E53DFB2668389659EDE.

Crowther, Bosley, '*The Thief of Bagdad*', *New York Times*, 6 December 1940, available online at: http://movies.nytimes.com/movie/review?res=9B03E6D91E3EE33ABC4E53DFB467838B659EDE.

Crowther, Bosley, '*Arabian Nights*', *New York Times*, 26 December 1942, available online at: http://movies.nytimes.com/movie/review?res=9C0CE1DC143FE33BBC4E51DFB4678389659EDE.

Davidson, Kelly, and John Hill, 'Under Control?: *Black Narcissus* and the Imagining of India', *Film Studies* no. 6, Summer 2005, pp. 1–12.

De Brunhoff, Jean, *The Story of Babar the Little Elephant*, trans. Merle S. Haas (New York: Random House, 1933).

deCordova, Richard, *Picture Personalities: The Emergence of the Star System in America* (Urbana: University of Illinois Press, 1990).

Dennis, Jeffery P., *We Boys Together: Teenagers in Love before Girl-Craziness* (Nashville, TN: Vanderbilt University Press, 2007).

Dixon, Winston Wheeler, *Lost in the Fifties: Recovering Phantom Hollywood* (Carbondale: Southern Illinois University Press, 2005).

Dorfman, Ariel, *The Empire's Old Clothes: What the Lone Ranger, Babar, and Other Innocent Heroes Do to Our Minds* (New York: Pantheon Books, 1983).

Doty, Alexander, *Making Things Perfectly Queer: Interpreting Mass Culture* (Minneapolis and London: University of Minnesota Press, 1993).

Drazin, Charles, *Korda: Britain's Only Movie Mogul* (London: Macmillan, 2002).

Drazin, Charles, 'Korda, Technicolor and the Zeitgeist', *Journal of British Cinema and Television* vol. 7 no. 1, April 2010, pp. 5–20.

Dyer, Richard, 'Resistance through Charisma: Rita Hayworth and *Gilda*', in E. Ann Kaplan (ed.), *Women in Film Noir* (London: BFI, 1980), pp. 91–9.

Dyer, Richard, *Heavenly Bodies: Film Stars and Society* (Basingstoke and London: Macmillan, 1986).

Edgecomb, Fredric, 'Camping Out with James Bidgood: The Auteur of *Pink Narcissus* Tells All', *Bright Lights Film Journal* no. 52, May 2006, available online at: http://www.brightlightsfilm.com/52/bidgoodiv.php (accessed 16 December 2013).

Eisele, John C., 'The Wild East: Deconstructing the Language of Genre in the Hollywood Eastern', *Cinema Journal* vol. 41 no. 4, Summer 2002, pp. 68–94.

Ellis, John, *Visible Fictions: Cinema, Television, Radio*, rev. edn (London and New York: Routledge, 1992 [1982]).

F. W., 'Elephant Boy', *Monthly Film Bulletin* vol. 4 no. 39, March 1937, p. 64.

Farmer, Brett, *Spectacular Passions: Cinema, Fantasy, Gay Male Spectatorships* (Durham, NC and London: Duke University Press, 2000).

Flaherty, David, 'Sabu', *World Film News* vol. 2 no. 1, April 1937, p. 11.

Flaherty, Frances Hubbard, *Elephant Dance* (London: Faber and Faber, 1937).

Flaherty, Frances and Ursula Leacock, *Sabu the Elephant Boy* (London: J. M. Dent and Sons, Ltd, 1937).

Flaherty, Robert, 'Mr. Flaherty and an Elephant Boy', *New York Times*, 10 November 1935, p. X4.

Ford, Phil, 'Time and Belief in Exotica', *Representations* vol. 103 no. 1, Summer 2008, pp. 107–35.

Gibbs, Henry, 'Shows Seen', *Action* no. 61, 17 April 1937, p. 13.

Gopinath, Gayatri, *Impossible Desires: Queer Diasporas and South Asian Public Cultures* (Durham, NC and London: Duke University Press, 2005).

Grierson, John, 'The Finest Eyes in Cinema', *World Film News* vol. 1 no. 12, March 1937, p. 5.

Guernsey Jr, Otis L., '*Cobra Woman*', *New York Herald Tribune*, 18 May 1944, reprinted in *New York Motion Picture Critics' Review 1944* vol. 1 no. 33, p. 370.

Haines, Richard W., *Technicolor Movies: The History of Dye Transfer Printing* (Jefferson, NC: McFarland and Co., 1993).

Hentzi, Gary, 'Little Cinema of Horrors', *Film Quarterly* vol. 46 no. 3, Spring 1993, pp. 22–7.

Hess, Gary R., 'The "Hindu" in America: Immigration and Naturalization Policies and India, 1917–1946,' *Pacific Historical Review* vol. 38 no. 1, February 1969, pp. 59–79.

Hess, Gary R., 'The Forgotten Asian Americans: The East Indian Company in the United States', *Pacific Historical Review* vol. 43 no. 4, November 1974, pp. 576–96.

Higgins, Scott, *Harnessing the Technicolor Rainbow: Colour Design in the 1930s* (Austin: University of Texas Press, 2007).

Hoberman, J., and Edward Leffingwell, (eds), *Wait for Me at the Bottom of the Pool: The Writings of Jack Smith* (New York and London: Serpent's Tail, 1997).

Hoberman, J., *On Jack Smith's* Flaming Creatures *and Other Secret-Flix of Cinemaroc* (New York: Hips Road, 2001).

Hobson, Harold, 'Man of Films', *The Christian Science Monitor*, 6 November 1935, p. 8.

Hollindale, Peter, *Signs of Childness in Children's Books* (Stroud: Thimble Press, 1997).

Howard, James, *Michael Powell* (London: B. T. Batsford, 1996).

Hutchison, Alice L., *Kenneth Anger: A Demonic Visionary* (London: Black Dog Publishing, 2004).

Hyam, Ronald, *Britain's Declining Empire: The Road to Decolonisation, 1918–1968* (Cambridge: Cambridge University Press, 2006).

Irwin, Robert, '*A Thousand and One Nights at the Movies*', *Middle Eastern Literatures* vol. 7 no. 2, July 2004, pp. 223–33.

Jaikumar, Priya, '"Place" and the Modernist Redemption of Empire in *Black Narcissus* (1947)', *Cinema Journal* vol. 40 no. 2, Winter 2001, pp. 57–77.

Jaikumar, Priya, *Cinema at the End of Empire: A Politics of Transition in Britain and India* (Durham, NC and London: Duke University Press, 2006).

Jennings, Wade, 'Nova: Garland in *A Star Is Born*,' *Quarterly Review of Film Studies* vol. 4 no. 3, Summer 1979, pp. 321–37.

Johnson, Dominic, 'The Deaths of Maria Montez', in *Glorious Catastrophe: Jack Smith, Performance and Visual Culture* (Manchester and New York: Manchester University Press, 2012), pp. 142–66.

Kipling, John Lockwood, *Beast and Man in India* (London and New York: Macmillan and Co., 1891).

Kipling, Rudyard, *Toomai of the Elephants* (London: Macmillan and Co., Ltd, 1937 [1894]).

Kipling, Rudyard, *The Jungle Book* (London: Penguin, 1987 [1894/1895]).

Koepnick, Lutz, 'Doubling the Double: Robert Siodmak in Hollywood', *New German Critique* no. 89, Spring–Summer 2003, pp. 81–104.

Korman, Seymour, 'Tigers, Women, and Love Won't Mix, Sabu Says', *Chicago Daily Tribune*, 17 October 1950, p. 4.

Kulik, Karol, *Alexander Korda: The Man Who Could Work Miracles* (London: Virgin Books, 1990 [1975]).

Lahiri, Shompa, *Indians in Britain: Anglo-Indian Encounters, Race and Identity, 1880–1930* (London and Portland, OR: Frank Cass, 2000).

Landy, Marcia, *British Genres: Cinema and Society, 1930–1960* (Princeton, NJ: Princeton University Press, 1991).

Lejeune, C. A., *Observer*, 19 July 1936, p. 12.

Lejeune, C. A., 'New Films in London', *The Times*, 6 September 1943, p. 8.

Lejeune, C. A., 'New Films in London', *The Times*, 23 December 1940, p. 6.

Lejeune, C. A., 'The Films', *Observer*, 22 December 1940, p. 3.

Levette, Harry, 'This Is Hollywood', *Chicago Defender*, 20 July 1946, p. 15.

Lury, Karen, *The Child in Film: Tears, Fears and Fairy Tales* (London and New York: I. B. Tauris, 2010).

MacKenzie, John M., *Propaganda and Empire: The Manipulation of British Public Opinion* (Manchester and New York: Manchester University Press, 1984).

McDonald, Paul, *The Star System: Hollywood's Production of Popular Identities* (London and New York: Wallflower, 2000).

McClintock, Anne, *Imperial Leather: Race, Gender and Sexuality in the Colonial Contest* (New York: Routledge, 1995).

McKernan, Luke, '"The Modern Elixir of Life": Kinemacolor, Royalty and the Delhi Durbar', *Film History* vol. 21 no. 2, Summer 2009, pp. 122–36.

McLean, Adrienne, and David A. Cook (eds), *Headline Hollywood: A Century of Film Scandal* (New Brunswick, NJ and London: Rutgers University Press, 2001).

McManus, John T., 'Sarongs Don't Make a Right', *New York Newspaper PM*, 18 May 1944, reprinted in *New York Motion Picture Critics' Review 1944* vol. 1 no. 33, p. 371.

Malamud, Randy, *Reading Zoos: Representations of Animals and Captivity* (New York: New York University Press, 1998).

Maltby, Richard, *Hollywood Cinema: An Introduction* (Oxford and Malden: Blackwell, 1995).

Misek, Richard, *Chromatic Cinema: A History of Screen Colour* (Chichester: Wiley-Blackwell, 2010).

Moon, Michael, 'Flaming Closets', *October* no. 51, Winter 1989, pp. 19–54.

Moor, Andrew, '*The Thief of Bagdad*: Arabian Fantasies', 26 May 2008, available online at: www.criterion.com/current/posts/496-the-thief-of-bagdad-arabian-fantasies.

Morgan, Guy, 'Take Your Family to See This Boy', *Daily Express*, 9 April 1937, p. 8.

Morgan, Guy, '*The Drum*', *Daily Express*, 6 April 1938, p. 10.

Morin, Edgar, *The Stars*, trans. Richard Howard (Minneapolis and London: University of Minnesota Press, 2005 [1972]).

Morse, Wilbur, Jr, '"Thief" of Bagdad (Sabu)', *Hollywood Magazine* vol. 28 no. 12, December 1939, pp. 32, 54.

Muñoz, José, *Disidentifications: Queers of Colour and the Performance of Politics* (Minneapolis and London: University of Minnesota Press, 1999).

Nandy, Ashis, 'The Psychology of Colonialism: Sex, Age and Ideology in British India', in Stephen Howe (ed.), *The New Imperial Histories Reader* (London and New York: Routledge, 2010), pp. 125–35.

Neale, Steve, *Cinema and Technology: Image, Sound, Colour* (London: BFI, 1985).

Newnham, John K., 'Sidelight on Sabu', *Film Weekly* vol. 20 no. 524, 29 October 1938, p. 23.

Nugent, Frank S., 'Elephant Boy', *New York Times*, 6 April 1937, available online at: http://movies.nytimes.com/movie/review?res=9906E7D6123AE23ABC4E53DFB 266838C629EDE.

O'Connor, Jim, 'Jungle Film at Criterion', *New York Journal-American*, 18 May 1944, reprinted in *New York Motion Picture Critics' Review 1944* vol. 1 no. 33, p. 371.

O'Harrow, Stephen, 'Babar and the *Mission Civilisatrice*: Colonialism and the Biography of a Mythical Elephant', *Biography* vol. 22 no. 1, Winter 1999, pp. 86–103.

Parsons, Louella, 'Sabu – the 1940 Thief of Bagdad – an Accomplished Actor', *Washington Post*, 20 October 1940, p. A1.

Patel, Baburao, Editorial, *Filmindia* vol. 4 no. 5, September 1938, p. 3.

Powdermaker, Hortense, *Hollywood: The Dream Factory: An Anthropologist Looks at the Movie-Makers* (Boston, MA: Little, Brown and Co., 1950).

Powell, Michael, *A Life in Movies: An Autobiography* (London: Heinemann, 1986).

Powell, Ryan, 'Dressing *Pink Narcissus*', in Marketa Uhlirova (ed.), *Birds of Paradise: Costume as Cinematic Spectacle* (London: Walther Koenig, 2013), pp. 305–16.

Prashad, Vijay, *The Karma of Brown Folk* (Minneapolis and London: University of Minnesota Press, 2000).

Provines, June, 'Front View and Profiles', *Chicago Daily Tribune*, 22 September 1938, p. 18.

Rashid, Ian Iqbal, 'Song of Sabu: Hollywood Cinema and the Displacement of Desire (Notes of the Film Script: Song of Sabu)', *Wasafiri* vol. 11 no. 23, 1996, pp. 33–9.

Richards, Frank, 'Aliens at Greyfriars', *Magnet* vol. 1 no. 6, 21 March 1908, no page.

Richards, Frank, 'The Greyfriars Gallery', *Magnet* vol. 11 no. 483, 12 May 1917, no page.

Richards, Jeffrey, *Visions of Yesterday* (London: Routledge, 1973).

Richards, Jeffrey, '"Patriotism with Profit": British Imperial Cinema in the 1930s', in James Curran and Vincent Porter (eds), *British Cinema History* (London: Weidenfeld and Nicolson, 1983), pp. 245–56.

Richards, Jeffrey, 'Boy's Own Empire: Feature Films and Imperialism in the 1930s', in John M. MacKenzie (ed.), *Imperialism and Popular Culture* (Manchester and New York: Manchester University Press, 1986), pp. 140–64.

Robbins, Paul, 'Pax Disney: The Annotated Diary of a Film Extra in India', in Tim Cresswell and Deborah Dixon (eds), *Engaging Film: Geographies of Mobility and Identity* (Lanham, MD: Rowman and Littlefield, 2002), pp. 159–73.

Roberts, Katherine, 'Civilizing Sabu of India: The Story of a Jungle Child in a Modern World', *Photoplay* vol. 53 no. 1, January 1939, p. 24.

Robson, W. W., 'Introduction', in Rudyard Kipling, *The Jungle Book* (Oxford and New York: Oxford University Press, 1987).

Ross, Andrew, *No Respect: Intellectuals and Popular Culture* (New York and London: Routledge, 1989).

Rotha, Paul, *Robert J. Flaherty: A Biography*, ed. Jay Ruby (Philadelphia: University of Pennsylvania Press, 1983).

Rózsa, Miklós, *Double Life: The Autobiography of Miklós Rózsa* (Tunbridge Wells/Midas Books; New York: Hippocrene Books, 1982).

Said, Edward, *Orientalism: Western Conceptions of the Orient* (London: Penguin, 1995 [1978]).

Sanderson, George Peress, *Thirteen Years among the Wild Beasts of India: Their Haunts and Habits from Personal Observations; With an Account of the Modes of Capturing and Taming Elephants* (London: W. H. Allen, 1879).

Schallert, Edwin, 'Sabu to Be 'Tough' in New Jungle Role', *Los Angeles Times*, 26 September 1938, p. 16.

Schickel, Richard, *His Picture in the Papers: A Speculation on Celebrity in America, Based on the Life of Douglas Fairbanks, Sr.* (New York: Charterhouse, 1973).

Sconce, Jeffrey, '"Trashing" the Academy: Taste, Excess, and an Emerging Politics of Cinematic Style', *Screen* vol. 36 no. 4, Winter 1995, pp. 371–93.

Sconce, Jeffrey, 'Dickens, Selznick and *Southpark*', in John Glavin (ed.), *Dickens on Screen* (Cambridge and New York: Cambridge University Press, 2003), pp. 171–87.

Shohat, Ella and Robert Stam, 'The Imperial Imaginary', in Graeme Turner (ed.), *The Film Cultures Reader* (London and New York: Routledge, 2002).

Shridharani, Krishnalal, *My India, My America*, with an introduction by Louis Bromfield (New York: Duell, Sloan and Pearce/Bombay: International Book House Ltd., 1941).

Shukla, Sandhya, *India Abroad: Diasporic Cultures of Postwar America and England* (Princeton, NJ and Oxford: Princeton University Press, 2003).

Small, Victor, 'Démarche of Time', *Left Review* vol. 3 no. 16, May 1938, pp. 1001–3.

Smith, Jack, 'The Perfect Filmic Appositeness of Maria Montez', in J. Hoberman and Edward Leffingwell (eds), *Wait for Me at the Bottom of the Pool: The Writings of Jack Smith* (New York and London: Serpent's Tail, 1997), pp. 25–36.

Smith, Jack, 'The Memoirs of Maria Montez or Wait for Me at the Bottom of the Pool', in J. Hoberman and Edward Leffingwell (eds), *Wait for Me at the Bottom of the Pool: The Writings of Jack Smith* (New York and London: Serpent's Tail, 1997), pp. 37–40.

Sontag, Susan, 'Notes on "Camp"', in *Against Interpretation and Other Essays* (London and New York: Penguin, 2009), pp. 275–92, originally published in *Partisan Review* vol. 31 no. 4, Fall 1964, pp. 515–30.

Stern, Lesley, and George Kouvaros, 'Descriptive Acts: Introduction', in Lesley Stern and George Kouvaros (eds), *Falling for You: Essays on Cinema and Performance* (Sydney: Power Publications, 1999), pp. 1–35.

Strauss, Theodore, 'New Arabian Nights: Sabu, The Elephant Boy, Today Travels via a Twin-motored Flying Carpet', *New York Times*, 15 September 1940, p. 35.

Street, Sarah, *British National Cinema* (London and New York: Routledge, 1997).

Street, Sarah, *Black Narcissus* (London and New York: I. B. Tauris, 2005).

Street, Sarah, *Colour Films in Britain: The Negotiation of Innovation, 1900–55* (London: BFI, 2012).

Tartaglia, Jerry, 'The Perfect Queer Appositeness of Jack Smith', *Quarterly Review of Film and Video* vol. 18 no. 1, 2001, pp. 39–52.

Taylor, Helen, *Scarlett's Women: Gone with the Wind and Its Female Fans* (New Brunswick, NJ: Rutgers University Press, 1989).

Thomas, Bob, 'Sabu, The Elephant Boy, Resumes Acting Career', *Hartford Courant*, 11 August 1957, p. 6.

Tinée, Mae, '*Elephant Boy* Good Film of Kipling Story', *Chicago Daily Tribune*, 9 June 1937, p. 17.

Turner, Graeme (ed.), *The Film Cultures Reader* (London and New York: Routledge, 2002).

Vidal, Gore, *Myra Breckinridge/Myron* (New York and London: Penguin Books, 1997 [1968, 1974]).

Visram, Rozina, *Asians in Britain: 400 Years of History* (London and Sterling, VA: Pluto Press, 2002).

Waller, Genevieve, 'Cobra Woman', *Quarterly Review of Film and Video* vol. 27 no. 5, October 2010, pp. 379–81.

Watson, Paul, 'There's No Accounting for Taste: Exploitation Cinema and the Limits of Film Theory', in Deborah Cartmell, I. Q. Hunter, Heidi Kaye and Imelda Whelehan (eds), *Trash Aesthetics: Popular Culture and Its Audience* (London and Chicago, IL: Pluto Press, 1997), pp. 66–83.

Waugh, Thomas, *The Romance of Transgression in Canada: Queering Sexualities, Nations, Cinemas* (Montreal and Ithaca, NY: McGill-Queen's University Press, 2006).

Weaver, Tom, *Eye on Science Fiction: 20 Interviews with Classic SF and Horror Filmmakers* (Jefferson, NC, and London: McFarland & Company, Inc., 2007).

Webster, Wendy, *Englishness and Empire 1939–1965* (Oxford: Oxford University Press, 2005).

Whittingham, Jack, *Sabu of the Elephants* (London: Hurst and Blackett, 1938).
Williams, Christopher (ed.), *Realism and the Cinema* (London and Henley: Routledge and Kegan Paul, 1980).
Williams, R. Ewart, 'Korda Begins a New Career', *Film Pictorial*, 10 December 1938, p. 13.
Yacowar, Maurice, 'An Aesthetic Defence of the Star System in Films', *Quarterly Review of Film Studies* vol. 4 no. 1, 1979, pp. 39–52.

Anonymous

'Bombay Calling', *Filmindia* vol. 20 no. 2, February 1954, p. 22.
Boy's Life vol. 27 no. 5, May 1937, p. 20.
Cinegram no. 25, 1938.
'*Cobra Woman*', *Today's Cinema* vol. 62 no. 5037, 26 May 1943, p. 20.
'Dancer at Sabu Trial Denies Affair in Egypt', *Los Angeles Times*, 14 October 1950, p. 10.
'Decision Reopens Case against Sabu', *Los Angeles Times*, 21 March 1952, p. 17.
'*The Drum*', *Manchester Guardian*, 6 April 1938, p. 96.
'Earl Carroll Spot Reopens,' *Billboard*, 13 January 1951, p. 42.
'*Elephant Boy*,' *Kinematograph Weekly* no. 1556, 11 February 1937, p. 34.
'*Elephant Boy*', *The Times*, 7 April 1937, p. 14.
'The Elephant Boy', *Manchester Guardian*, 15 March 1937, p. 14.
'"Elephant Boy" of Films Now Gunner on Plane', *New York Times*, 16 February 1945, p. 4.
'"Elephant Boy" Sabu Dies of Heart Attack,' *Los Angeles Times*, 3 December 1963, p. 2.
'"*Elephant Boy*'s' Success', *Manchester Guardian*, 15 March 1937, p. 12.
'"Elephant Boy" Returns', *Times of India*, 20 October 1953, p. 3.
'"*Elephant Boy*" Unit's Adventures', *Kinematograph Weekly* no. 1487, 17 October 1935, p. 58.
'Elephants Like His Smile,' *Daily Mirror*, 9 December 1935, p. 8.
'English Dancer Accuses Sabu as Father of Child', *Los Angeles Times*, 24 May 1949, p. 2.
Exhibitor's Campaign Book for *The Drum*, 1938.
'Film Expedition in Search of "Elephant Boy",' *Times of India*, 2 February 1935, p. 17.
Film Pictorial vol. 12 no. 297, 30 October 1937, p. 4.
Film Pictorial vol. 13 no. 232, 23 April 1938, pp. 16–17 (Tom Sawyer reference).
Filmindia vol. 3 no. 11, March 1938.
Filmindia vol. 4 no. 5, September 1938.
Filmindia vol. 5 no. 2, February 1939.
Filmindia vol. 5 no. 9, September 1939.
Filmindia vol. 18 no. 9, September 1952.
Filmindia vol. 20 no. 3, March 1954.

Filmindia vol. 20 no. 4, April 1954.

Filmindia vol. 20 no. 5, May 1954.

Filmindia vol. 20 no. 6, June 1954.

'The Films Provide a Christmas Pantomime', *Picture Post* vol. 9 no. 11, 14 December 1940, p. 31.

'Harringay Arena: Tom Arnold's Circus', *The Times*, 21 December 1951, p. 2.

'A Hero of Modern Arabian Nights', *Screen Thrills Illustrated* vol. 2 no. 4, May 1964, pp. 29–33.

'Hunt for India's Boy Film Star', *Times of India*, 9 March 1935, p. 19.

'Impressive Kipling Film at Empire', *Times of India*, 12 June 1937, p. 7.

'Indian Boy as Kim Hero', *Observer*, 27 January 1935, p. 10.

'Indian Boy Screen Star', *Times of India*, 2 December 1936, p. 17.

'*Jaguar*', *Variety*, 23 April 1956, no page.

'*Jungle Book*', *Kinematograph Weekly* no. 1834, 11 June 1942, p. 20.

'Jungle Friends Didn't Forget', *Daily Mirror*, 21 June 1937, p. 5.

'Kipling Film in Colour: *Jungle Book*', *The Times*, 4 June 1942, p. 6.

'A Kipling Jungle Is Re-created', *New York Times Magazine*, 8 March 1942, p. 14.

'Korda's Brilliant Film of Kipling's *The Jungle Book*', *Today's Cinema* vol. 58 no. 4732, 5 June 1942, pp. 1, 27.

'The Life Story of Sabu,' *Picture Show* vol. 48 no. 1229, 29 January 1944, p. 11.

'Lived in Sabu's Room, Dancer Says in Court', *Chicago Daily Tribune*, 11 October 1950, p. 9.

'Mr. Korda's Plans – A New Eastern Cycle', *Manchester Guardian*, 16 June 1938, p. 12.

Morning Telegraph, New York, 23 August 1941, no page.

'New Film of India', *Times of India*, 11 February 1936, p. 8.

'New Films in London', *The Times*, 23 December 1940, p. 6.

'New Films in London', *The Times*, 25 January 1943, p. 8.

'New Films in London', *The Times*, 6 September 1943, p. 8.

'Palace to Become Cinema Studio', *Times of India*, 2 July 1935, p. 5.

'Rooney Firm Plans Three Film Series', *Billboard*, 10 July 1954, p. 7.

'Rooney Preps *Tokyo*, *Magic Lamp* Kickoffs', *Billboard*, 24 July 1954, pp. 7, 31.

'Sabu', *Western Mail*, 29 September 1936, p. 3.

'Sabu as an Indian Prince in a Colourful Story of the North-West Frontier', *Film Pictorial* vol. 13 no. 320, 9 April 1938, pp. 14–15, 25.

'Sabu at the Zoo', *Daily Mirror*, 6 April 1937, p. 6.

'Sabu Dastagir, Movies' Elephant Boy, Dies at 39', *Washington Post*, 4 December 1963, p. 15.

'Sabu Denies Paternity but Agrees to Aid Child', *Los Angeles Times*, 16 July 1953, p. 15.

'Sabu: Elephant Boy of the Films', *The Times*, 4 December 1963, p. 18.
'Sabu, Former Child Actor, DFC Winner', *Washington Post*, 8 March 1945, p. 2.
'Sabu, on Stand, Denies Being Father of Child', *Los Angeles Times*, 17 October 1950, p. 8.
'Sabu's Smile', *Times of India*, 30 December 1936, p. 10.
'Sabu the Elephant Boy Is Dead', *New York Times*, 3 December 1963, p. 43.
'Sabu, This Is Billy!', *Daily News, New York*, 18 September 1938, page unknown.
Saturday Review no. 4306, 16 April 1938, p. 242.
'Search for Boy to Take Part of Mahout's Son', *Times of India*, 29 March 1935, p. 12.
'She's Colourful', *Film Pictorial* vol. 10 no. 238, 12 September 1938, p. 14.
'The Social Whirl: Elephant Boy Comes to Town', *Times of India*, 25 October 1953, p. 11.
The Story of United Artists Product 1937–1938: The Book of the Year, 1939.
'Studio and Screen', *Manchester Guardian*, 25 February 1937, p. 12.
'Surf Sets up Taj Mahal Co', *Billboard*, 2 October 1954, p. 2.
'Tea from the Empire', *The Times*, 11 January 1939, p. 7.
'*The Thief of Bagdad*', *Picture Show*, 8 March 1941, p. 17.
'Verdict of Jury Clears Sabu in Paternity Suit', *Los Angeles Times*, 19 October 1950, pp. 1, 12.
'The Week at the Zoo', *Observer*, 25 April 1937, p. 15.
'When Darkness Falls', *Film Pictorial* vol. 10 no. 241, 3 October 1936, p. 8.
'When East Meets West End', *Australian Women's Weekly*, 22 May 1937, p. 51.
'Where Are Britain's New Stars?', *Film Pictorial* vol. 10 no. 248, 21 November 1936, p. 7.

Filmography

Elephant Boy (Robert Flaherty, Zoltan Korda, UK, 1937)
The Drum (Zoltan Korda, UK, 1938)
The Thief of Bagdad (Ludwig Berger, Michael Powell, Tim Whelan, UK, 1940)
Jungle Book (Zoltan Korda, UK, 1942)
Arabian Nights (John Rawlins, US, 1942)
White Savage (Arthur Lubin, US, 1943)
Cobra Woman (Robert Siodmak, US, 1944)
Tangier (George Waggner, US, 1946)
Black Narcissus (Michael Powell, Emeric Pressburger, UK, 1947)
The End of the River (Derek N. Twist, UK, 1947)
Man-eater of Kumaon (Byron Haskin, US, 1948)
Song of India (Albert S. Rogell, US, 1949)
Savage Drums (William Berke, US, 1951)
Buongiorno, elefante! (Gianni Franciolini, Italy, 1952)
Il tesoro del Bengala (Gianni Vernuccio, Italy, 1953)
The Black Panther (Ron Ormond, US, 1956)
Jaguar (George Blair, US, 1956)
Jungle Hell (Norman A. Cerf, US, 1956)
Sabu and the Magic Ring (George Blair, US, 1957)
Die Herrin der Welt (William Dieterle, France/Italy/West Germany, 1960)
Rampage (Phil Karlson, US, 1963)
A Tiger Walks (Norman Tokar, US, 1964)

Index

Page numbers in **bold** denote detailed analysis; those in *italic* denote illustrations.
$n =$ endnote.

Andy's Gang 107
Anger, Kenneth 21*n*60
Ansari, Humayan 8*n*12
Anstey, F. 40
Arabian Nights (1942) 69, 71, 76, **79–81**, *81*, 89, 101
Arnold, Tom 93
Ashcroft, Bill 34, 35

Babar the Elephant *see The Story of Babar the Little Elephant*
Baboo Hurry Bungsho Jabberjee, BA London 40
babu 40
Babuscio, Jack 79
Balász, Béla 27
Barsam, Richard 12
Bartholomew, Freddie 14, 19, 27, 27*n*68
Basten, Fred E. 46, 48–9,
Beast and Man in India (Kipling) 9–10

Berger, John 29
Berry, Sarah 46
Bhabha, Homi K. 48
Bidgood, James 74–5
Biro, Lajos 12
Black Narcissus (1947) 74, 91, 94
Blaut, J. M. 8
Bomba the Jungle Boy 107
Borradaile, Osmond *15*, 16, *20*
Bride of the Monster (1955) 105
Bruce, David 108
Bunter, Billy 40
Buongiorno, Elefante! (1952) 93
Burmese Silver (Thompson) 52
Burton, Tim 105
Butler, Jeremy 5

Cabal, Robert 109
Calder-Marshall, Arthur 11–12

Calleia, Joseph 67
Captain's Courageous (1937) 27*n*68
chimpanzee
  in *Cobra Woman* 86, 88–9
Chiquita 103
Chowdhry, Prem 53, 53–4
circus 93–4
Clive of India (1935) 49
Cobra Woman (1944) 69, 71, 77, **86–9**, *87*, 106
Collier, John 12
colonialism 8, 29, 33–7
  and Babar the Elephant 34–6, 39
  and *The Drum* 52–5, 97
Connors, Touch 103, 105
Cooper, Marilyn 93, 94
crocodiles
  in *Jaguar* 103
  in *Jungle Book* 63
  in *Jungle Hell* 110
Crowther, Bosley 61, 62, 63

INDEX

Dastagir, Jasmine 93
Dastagir, Paul 93, 96, 108
David Copperfield (1935) 14
David Livingstone (1936) 49
De Brunhoff, Jean 34
De Camp, Rosemary 64
deCordova, Richard 94
Dennis, Jeffrey P. 76, 85
De Sica, Vittorio 93
Dorfman, Ariel 34, 35
Drazin, Charles 45, 57
The Drum (1938) 21, 29, 36, 38–9, *44*, 45, **49–56**, *50*, 60, 97
Dunna, Steffi 47
Duprez, June 58
Durbin, Deanna 21*n*61
Dyer, Richard 55–6, 78, 79, 90

Ed Wood (1994) 105
elephants 1, 9–10, 29–32, 93–4
  in *Elephant Boy* 10, 12, 16–17, 21–2
  in *Jungle Book* 67–8
  in *Jungle Hell* 109–12
Elephant Boy (1937) 3, *6*, **7–28**, 33, 35, 37, 43, 45, 49, 51, 53, 67, 96, 100, 105, 108, 112, 113
Elephant Dance (Flaherty) 11, 13, 16, 27
Ellis, John 5
Erikson, Leif 79

Farmer, Brett 79
Filmindia 36, 53, 96–9
Flaherty, David 14, 37, 53
Flaherty, Frances 11, 13, 16, 17, 19, 27, 28, 29, 34
Flaherty, Robert 11–14, 17, 20–3, 25–6, 112, 113
Fleming, Victor 27*n*68
Ford, John 27*n*68
Four Feathers (1939) 49
Four Men and a Prayer (1938) 49
Franklin, Pamela 113

Garland, Judy 78, 90
Gilbert, Billy 80
Gone with the Wind (1939) 14*n*39
Grable, Betty 71
The Great Barrier (1936) 49
Grierson, John 22
Gunga Din (1939) 49, 53*n*196

Hale, Jonathan 103
Hall, Jon 71, 79, 81, 85, 86, 107
Haver, June 45
Henie, Sonja 41*n*142, 93
Hentzi, Gary 101
Higgins, Scott 47–8
Hollindale, Peter 61–2
Howard, Shemp 79, 80
Hudd, Walter 26

Hurree Jamset Ram Singh 40–1
Hurry Bungsho Jabberjee 41; *see also Baboo Hurry Bungsho Jabberjee, BA London*
Huxley, Julian 29
Hyam, Ronald 33*n*97

ice-skating 41, 63, 93–4, 121*n*142

Jaguar (1956) 32, 69, 88, 100, **101–7**, *102*
Jaikumar, Priya 54, 74
Jennings, Wade 78
jiu jitsu 63–4
The Jungle Book (Kipling) 9, 29, 52
Jungle Book (1942) 32, 49, 52, **62–9**, *65*, 88, 100, 106, 110
Jungle Boy 107
Jungle Hell (1956) **107–13**, *111*
Jungle Jim 107
Justin, John 58, *61*

Kaa (*Jungle Book*) 66–7, 89, 106
Kalmus, Herbert 45
Kendall, Bobby 74–5
King Solomon's Mines (1937) 49
Kipling, Lockwood 9
Kipling, Rudyard 9

Korda, Alexander 11–13, 20–1, 45, 51, 53, 57, 91, 97
Korda, Zoltan 12–13, 23, 112
Kouvaros, George 5
Kracauer, Siegfried 11
Kulik, Karol 12

Lahiri, Shompa 40
Lamour, Dorothy 71
Landy, Marcia 57n206, 58
Leacock, Ursula 34
Lejeune, C. A. 42, 57, 59
Lives of a Bengal Lancer (1935) 49
Livesey, Roger 38, 54
Lombard, Carol 37
London Films 11, 51
London Zoo 29
Lugosi, Bela 71, 105
Lury, Karen 27

McClintock, Anne 36
MacKenzie, John M. 49
MacLane, Barton 103
McLean, Adrienne L. 95
The Magic Lamp see Sabu and the Magic Ring
Maltby, Richard 78

Man-Eater of Kumaon (1948) 32, 91
Massey, Raymond 55
A Midsummer Night's Dream (Shakespeare) 20–1

A Midsummer Night's Dream (1935) 21n60
Misek, Richard 48
Mitchum, Robert 113
mongoose 29
monkeys
  in *Elephant Boy* 21–2
  biting Sabu 29
Montez, Maria 71, 73, 77–8, 79, 81, 85, 86
Moon, Michael 73
Moor, Andrew 58, 61
Morin, Edgar 4
Mother India (1957) 96
Muñoz, José 90

Naji 108
Nandy, Ashis 34
Nanook of the North (1922) 11
Neale, Steve 47
Nimmi 99

octopuses
  in *The Thief of Bagdad* 1
  rubber 105
O'Harrow, Stephen 34–5, 39
orientalism 51
O'Rourke, Patricia 69

Pal 45
Parsons, Louella 53
Patel, Baburao 53
piglet 106
Pink Narcissus (1971) 74–5

Powell, Michael 52, 57, 74
Powell, Ryan 75n246
Prashad, Vijay 29
The Private Life of Henry VIII (1933) 11

Qualen, John 80

Ramar of the Jungle 107
Rampage (1963) 113
Republic Pictures 101
Rhodes of Africa (1936) 49
Richards, Frank 40
Richards, Jeffrey 39, 49, 51
Rikki, Sabu's pet mongoose 29
Robbins, Paul 79
Rooney, Mickey 21n61, 101, 113
Ross, Andrew 72–3
Rotha, Paul 13, 22
Rózsa, Miklós 4

Sabu and the Magic Ring (1957) *92*, 101–2
Sabu of the Elephants (Whittingham) 10, 32, 36, 39, 41, 51–2
Sabu the Elephant Boy (Flaherty and Leacock) 34, 35
Sahu, Kishore 96, 99
Said, Edward 51
Sande, Sarena 108
Sanders of the River (1935) 49

Sanderson, George 9
Sauda 96–9
Sconce, Jeffrey 100
Selznick, David 14, 14*n*39
Shashikala 97–9
Sheffield, Johnny 107–8
Shere Khan (*Jungle Book*)
    62, 63–7, 110
Shohat, Ella 52
smile 4, 8, 16, 17, 25, 26,
    28, 37, 54–6, 58, 60,
    66–7, 97, 113
Smith, Jack 74, 77–8
snake
   in *Jaguar* 104–6
   see also Kaa
Song of India (1949) 69,
    91–2
Stam, Robert 52
Stanhope, Ted 109
Stanley and Livingstone
    (1939) 49
Stern, Lesley 5
Stevens, K. T. 109
The Story of Babar the
    Little Elephant 34–6,
    39 *see also*
    colonialism

Street, Sarah 46, 49–50,
    52–3, 54

Tartaglia, Jerry 73–4
Tarzan 62, 63, 107
Technicolor 3, 21, 43,
    45–69, 71, 77–8, 89
Temple, Shirley 8, 17, 19,
    27*n*68
Tester, Desmond 55, *56*
The Thief of Bagdad 1, *2*,
    49, 52, 56, **57–62**, *61*,
    68–9, 74, **75–7**, 80,
    81, 93, 101
Thirteen Years among the
    Wild Beasts of India
    (Sanderson) 9
Thompson, Captain *38*,
    39, 41
Thompson, Edward John
    52
The Tiger of Eschnapur
    (1938) 53*n*196
A Tiger Walks (1964) 32,
    113
'Toomai of the Elephants'
    9
Trader Horn (1931) 49

turban 4, 23, *24*, 36, 37,
    42, 47

United Artists 51
Universal Studios 49, 71,
    91

Venice Film Festival 13
Veidt, Conrad 58
Visram, Rozina 8*n*12

Waller, Genevieve 73
Watson, Paul 100
Wee Willie Winkie (1937)
    27*n*68
Weissmuller, Johnny 27,
    63, 107
White Savage (1943) 70,
    71, 78, **81–5**, 86, 88
Whittingham, Jack 10, 32,
    36, 36–7, 39, 41, 51–2
The Winter's Tale
    (Shakespeare) 61
Wood, Ed 105
World War II 3, 45, 71, 91,
    99

Yacowar, Maurice 3, 4

List of Illustrations

While considerable effort has been made to correctly identify the copyright holders, this has not been possible in all cases. We apologise for any apparent negligence and any omissions or corrections brought to our attention will be remedied in any future editions.

The Thief of Bagdad, © Alexander Korda Film Productions; *Elephant Boy*, London Film Productions; *The Drum*, London Film Productions; *Jungle Book*, Alexander Korda Films Inc.; *White Savage*, © Universal Pictures Company Inc.; *Cobra Woman*, © Universal Pictures Company; *Sabu and the Magic Ring*, Allied Artists Pictures Corporation; *Jaguar*, Republic Pictures Corporation; *Jungle Hell*, Taj Mahal Productions; *Arabian Nights*, Universal Pictures Company.